FILM FLUBS

FILM FLUBS

Memorable Movie Mistakes

BILL GIVENS

A CITADEL PRESS BOOK
PUBLISHED BY CAROL PUBLISHING GROUP

A Citadel Press Book
Published by Carol Publishing Group
Citadel Press is a registered trademark of Carol Communications, Inc.

Editorial, sales and distribution, rights and permissions inquiries should be addressed to Carol Publishing Group, 120 Enterprise Avenue, Secaucus, N.J. 07094

In Canada: Canadian Manda Group, One Atlantic Avenue, Suite 105, Toronto, Ontario M6K 3E7

Carol Publishing Group books may be purchased in bulk at special discounts for sales promotion, fund-raising, or educational purposes. Special editions can be created to specifications. For details, contact Special Sales Department, 120 Enterprise Avenue, Secaucus, N.J. 07094.

Manufactured in the United States of America

10 9 8 7 6 5 4 3 2 1

Library of Congress Cataloging-in-Publication Data
Givens, Bill.
  Film Flubs : memorable movie mistakes / Bill Givens.
    p. cm.
  "Updated."
  "A Citadel Press book."
  Includes index.
  ISBN (invalid) 0-8065-2053-3 (pbk.)
  1. Motion pictures—Humor. 2. Motion picture errors. I. Title.
PN1994.9.G58 1998
791.43'75'0207—dc21   98-34001
                                                          CIP

CONTENTS

INTRODUCTION
Welcome to *Film Flubs*—the 1999 Edition!

Once upon a time, there was a book called *Film Flubs*. It was quite a hit with film fans, who wanted to share the goofs, gaffes, and slipups they'd spotted in their favorite movies. They were generous with their cards and letters listing the flubs they'd found, so along came *Son of Film Flubs*, then *Film Flubs: The Sequel*. A few years passed, and, as often happens in the world of books, the earlier titles became difficult to find. This led to a new book: *Roman Soldiers Don't Wear Watches*, incorporating a brand-new collection of flubs along with favorites from the earlier volumes.

But the cards, letters, and e-mails continued to roll in, many from readers who hadn't seen the earlier volumes. So we're back with *Film Flubs*, the 1999 edition, with more than one hundred new flubs along with a collection of classics which didn't appear in *Roman Soldiers Don't Wear Watches*. We hope you'll enjoy this melange of the old and new. Many of the newer flubs appeared in films released during 1996 through 1998. If you didn't spot them when the films appeared in the theaters, now's your chance, as many have been released on video.

It's always a joy to hear from the thousands of film buffs who enjoy this series of books. The volume of mail is overwhelming, far more than we can respond to personally. One of our long-term life goals is to respond to all of the generous people who share with us the flubs they've spotted. (Keeping this as a goal may well be one way to ensure a long life.)

Nowadays, we hear from you within days of a movie's release if there's a flub in it. The instantaneous and ever-changing nature of modern communications has resulted in much of our correspondence changing from letters to e-mails, which we admit facilitates an easy response. So maybe we'll be better at it. Please continue to write to bgivens@earthlink.net, or click the mail form on our home page, http://www.home.earthlink.net/~bgivens. A filmflubs.com site is underway as of this writing as well. Of course, the good old postal address is still fine, too: Film Flubs, 7510 Sunset Boulevard #551, Los Angeles, CA 90046.

Speaking of the mail: Most of the letters we've received have had to do with two instances of something mysterious seeming to have happened on film. They're the stuff of urban rumors, tales that get better and more mysterious with each telling. One involved the "ghost kid" in *Three Men and a Baby* (1987). We delved into that one pretty deeply in *Son of Film Flubs* and *Roman Soldiers Don't Wear Watches,* so there's not much that we can add about that here. We still continue to get letters from readers who agree with our conclusions, but there's no dearth of those who disagree. There's apparently no way to be definitive about the flub, hard as we try. If you believe in ghosts, it's there. If you don't, it isn't. More often than not, the flub is in the eye of the beholder.

The other flub about which we get reams and reams of mail is the "apparent suicide" in *The Wizard of Oz* (1939). Again, we are fully convinced that it didn't happen, and tried to say so. True, something is moving in the background when Dorothy and her friends first head down the yellow brick road. After checking a couple of video versions, we said that even though we were sure there was no suicide on the set, it appeared that we were seeing a crew member moving around. But many of you checked it out for yourselves and most came up with the same conclusion as we did after later seeing a sharper copy on laser disc: it's a bird. A big bird, wandering around the forest.

On their Web site, MGM acknowledges that they continue to receive letters about the "incident," some viewers claiming that they see it in Munchkinland, while others see it in the forest scenery. They also cite the *Film Flubs* books as well as a mention of it in *Roger Ebert's Video Companion*, 1994 edition, page 828. They say, "A resident Oz expert here in the office has given what we think is the scene a close look and the most he could find is a large, colorful bird toward the rear of the forest set, a bird that viewers might be interpreting as the mystery hanged man." But some continue to believe the suicide rumor even though, as we said in the earlier books, "C'mon now. Do you think if that was indeed the case, Hollywood could have kept it quiet all these years? This is a town where everything is public knowledge. Everything." (*Roman Soldiers,* p. 159.) So until and unless some new evidence comes to life, we'll leave it at that. If the conclusions you draw are otherwise, *chaçon à son gout.*

This collection encompasses new flubs from some of the blockbuster movies of the last several years, including a selection from the record-setting *Titanic* (1997). It shows that no matter how thorough your research (and *Titanic's* filmmakers were meticulous in theirs), little glitches can slip through. It's fun to find them, fun to share them, and the most fun we have comes in the appreciative letters we receive from our wonderful readers. Enjoy this collection, and look for more of the series in the future!

FILM FLUBS

ASPECTS OF THE BOOM TIMES

The most often noticed film flub is the appearance of a boom mike on screen. Perhaps more than any other glitch, a roving mike in the frame has the potential to grab your attention and distract you from the story or the onscreen action.

You should know that it's important to keep the boom mike as close as possible to the actors in order to get a good strong voice track—even though much of the track will be redone in the studio during a "looping" session—as well as to minimize outside noise. Essentially, two types of booms are used in films—a rolling boom, on which the mike is manipulated with pulleys and cables, and the more popular "fishpole" boom. The boom operator stands just outside the frame, holding the mike on a long fiberglass pole just over the actor's heads, moving it back and forth from speaker to speaker. The mike that some viewers see sneaking into the frame is usually a long tubular device, covered with either a foam or a shaggy fabric wind screen.

Oddly, one person may see a boom mike in a particular theater or in a television broadcast, while another may never see it—because it's not always there. This has to do with the many variations on the size and projection of the picture.

Since the beginning of the movie industry, there has been constant experimentation with screen size and masking, with camera and projector technology, and with projection booth automation. Add to this mix the possibility of human error (especially when today's projectionist might be a button-pushing high schooler in a computerized mall multiplex) and the chances of visible onscreen mishaps increase by quantum leaps.

The configuration of the picture you see on the screen is known as the *aspect ratio*. This is the relationship of the height of the screen to its width. Early filmmakers produced a picture that was relatively square, which evolved into what is now known as the "Academy Aperture." The width of the picture was about one third larger than the height, for a ratio of 1.33:1. It's still the shape of the frame on 35mm film. In the early 1950s, CinemaScope came along, with 2.35:1 ratio. Many theaters jumped onto the new standard—since all it involved was installation of a new screen and some new lenses for the projectors—as opposed to 3-D and Cinerama, which required a complete refitting. CinemaScope was shot on the same 35mm stock, but it was filmed through an anamorphic camera lens. This squeezed the picture onto the film and then, when shown through a similar anamorphic projection lens, it was spread back out on the screen. Since the CinemaScope patent was tightly held and distribution rigidly controlled, competitive systems quickly emerged—including some in which the top and bottom strips of the film frame were not used, with the middle, wide-shaped segment being magnified out to ratios such as 1.85:1, the size you see most often on today's screens. In some instances, the top and bottom strips were masked off; in others, the area was just not used for picture, giving ample room for boom mikes and all sorts of other things to roam around the top of the frame.

Another development was 70mm, which gave greater clarity on large screens for "road show" (reserved seats) engagements, and was then reduced to 35 mm CinemaScope for general release. It's still in use today, with some of the mega-pictures—such as Disney's recent restoration of *Fantasia* (1940) going out in both road show and wide-screen formats. One of the major advantages of 70mm is that it carries a magnetic sound track, vastly improving the sound quality. Also just emerging is digital sound, which takes film into the sound quality range of compact discs.

The number of film formats used over the years is awesome, and it's daunting to try and understand them. A few names: MetroScope, MegaScope, CinemaScope, VistaVision, WarnerScope, Camerascope, SuperScope, Tohoscope, Hammerscope, TechniScope, Franscope, Todd-AO, Camera 65, Cinerama 70, Vitascope, Vitarama, Super Technirama, Cinemiracle, and Panavision.

With all of the projection size possibilities, it's up to the local theater to properly mask its screen to give the image its best frame. If the masking is off or the projector framing slightly askew, there just might be some things at the top or bottom of the frame that the filmmakers didn't intend for you to see.

The better theaters have adjustable masking; they can move the black borders on the four sides of the screen to accommodate the proper aspect ratio of the particular film being shown. Others can move the side borders in and out, but the top and bottom bands are stationary. And still others—probably the majority—can't adjust their masking at all.

There are a few other elements to the aspect situation. One is the aperture plate in the projector. Quite frequently, unless the theater owner or projectionist cares enough (or knows enough) to change the aperture plate in the projector—the frame through which the film is projected—and adjust screen masking, a pre-1950s movie will be projected with the top and bottom lopped off. Heads and feet fall by the wayside, to say nothing of what happens to the director and cinematographer's careful compositions. You might even have the experience of seeing more than the director wanted to reveal to you—such as John Denver's shorts, which show in an improper framing when he comes out of the shower in *Oh, God!* (1977).

Another cause of the microphone sneaking onto the screen is that often directors and script supervisors are watching the scene through a *video assist,* as it is being filmed. The camera operator is the only person who can see exactly what the lens is seeing, and he has to think about focus, lighting, all sorts of things. To enable others in the crew to see exactly what the camera's eye sees, either a small video camera is placed atop the film camera, or the film camera itself has a video tap, with a TV monitor elsewhere on the set. Quite often something out of the ordinary can be seen when it comes into the frame. But the picture is not as clear as that on your home TV set. Lighting on the set is designed for the film camera, not for the monitor, so things can slip right past, things like microphone intrusions.

Now, let's venture into another minefield. Until the home video explosion, movies were made to be shown in movie theaters, for better or worse. Television was at first no consideration, then only a minor one. Now it's a major consideration. Most movies will make a quick trip into the home video market, some within days of their theatrical release. (I recall commenting to a friend when we were leaving the press preview of the movie I consider the hands-down winner as the worst of 1990, *Fire Birds,* "This turkey will be in the video stores before we get home tonight!")

At any rate, when a wide-screen movie is converted for television or home video use, there's no way the entire image can be seen on a television screen—unless the picture is "letterboxed," the method preferred by most film buffs as well as by the directors and cinematographers who worked so hard to create a specific onscreen experience. But the letterbox, with its black bands at the top and bottom of the TV picture, creates a relatively small image on the screen. This naturally takes away some of the intimacy of the image unless you have a mega-monitor or projection TV.

So most films are "panned and scanned." (The pan, incidentally, has nothing to do with the way it was reviewed by the critics!) A video operator scans the film, panning back and forth across the wide image to record the relatively square portion of the picture that will appear on your TV when you run the videocassette. Rarely are the craftsmen who made the film involved with it in the studio during this process, and the meticulously-composed work of a world-class director or cinematographer is left to the judgment of a video technician.

"Pan and scan" produces some Hollywood horror stories—leaving an actor in what was originally a two-shot talking to thin air, or, as in one of the Fred Astaire-Ginger Rogers movies where Ginger dances right off the screen and back on again. That certainly wasn't in the director's plan.

The next time you see a "letterboxed" movie on TV or videocassette, imagine what you'd be seeing if you had to select only about two-thirds of the picture. That's what happens when it's panned and scanned. And that's what happened particularly to Gene Kelly and Stanley Donen's wonderful 1955 *It's Always Fair Weather,* when Kelly's meticulously choreographed "Ash Can Dance" featuring Michael Kidd, Dan Dailey and himself performing in three side-by-side screen panels was completely destroyed when only two-thirds of the scene could be accommodated in the panned and scanned version for TV.

When the film is converted to TV, there's a good chance that the errant mike boom and other glitches and gaffes that were seen on the theater screen are caught by the video operator and cut out of the picture—or, due to the exigencies of the "home cutoff" on various TV sets (the picture you see at home is about a half-inch smaller all the way around than the one on TV studio monitors), may or may not be in the home video or broadcast versions. The lesson is that while boom intrusions are the most frequent of film flubs, the mike you see may not be seen by someone else, unless of course it's way into the frame.

A recent example of a flub being lost to "pan and scan" is in *The Two Jakes* (1990). When Jack Nicholson is going into a beauty salon in a scene set in the late 1940s, in the theatrical version of the film a Bank of America automatic teller machine can be seen in the background—something that didn't exist at the time of the film. But in the home video version, there's just a hint of the machine at the right side of the frame.

The purpose of this little dissertation is not so much to reveal the mike boom film flubs (don't leave—they're coming), but to give me the opportunity to preach my particular sermon—that most movies should be seen in theaters.

Shortly after *FILM FLUBS* was published, I took some heat from home video magazines and video rental stores about my statement that "the only real way to see a movie remains on a big screen in a real movie theater." Even though I'm as good a customer as the video business will ever have, I stand by my guns.

With the exception of made-for-television films and some low-budget turkeys, movies are made to be seen on the big screen. Not only do you get the best visual presentation (hopefully), but you become part of the shared audience experience.

I know many film critics who prefer to do their viewing in an audience setting, rather than by themselves in a screening room. The effect of shared laughter and tears, suspense and terror, beauty and excitement, is very much a part of the moviegoing experience. Movies are made to be seen by audiences, and seeing a movie in a crowded theater on a big screen can only heighten the experience.

Besides, who can really enjoy a movie without fresh popcorn? Microwave popcorn, as much as I love it, isn't worth the butter it's cooked in.

Just hope that you can find one of the few theaters where the operators really *care* about films and their exhibition, where the floors aren't sticky or smelly, and the seats comfortable. Sadly, it's becoming a quixotic quest.

At the risk of treading on some toes of very good friends in the movie business, I have to say this: When you want to see a really important film or one that has some special meaning for you, seek out the biggest and best theater that you can find, preferably a single-screen house. If you are lucky enough to have nearby an old movie palace, restored or otherwise, that's not playing action/adventure trash movies, go see it there. Go, even if, as in Los Angeles and many other major cities, the film you want to see is running with foreign-language subtitles. You might learn a new language!

One of my close friends produced the landmark *Altered States* (1980). I first saw it in a movie house with the sound system set up to the producer and director's specifications. Later, I saw it on cable television and home video. It's virtually two different movies.

We were discussing the film recently, and agreed that the film loses about two-thirds of its power on television. In the movie theater, with its big screen and powerful sound system, *Altered States* will literally peel your skin off. Roger Ebert said in his review, "I can tell myself that this movie is a fiendishly constructed visual and verbal roller coaster, a movie deliberately intended to overwhelm its audiences with sensual excess. I know all that, and yet I *was* overwhelmed, I *was* caught up in its headlong energy." He's absolutely right, and the film itself is one of the best demonstrations of the reason movies should first be seen on the big screen.

An Ivy League college student son of some friends told me he had been going to movies all of his life, but he'd never seen one in any theater other than a shopping-mall multiplex. After having viewed *Gone With the Wind* several times on television and once at a multiplex, the night before

our conversation he had seen the restored *GWTW* print perfectly projected at a special screening in a magnificently-restored large-screen movie palace. He was absolutely dazzled by the experience. Not only did the film itself take on an entirely new meaning and depth, but he had no idea that a movie could look like that and could have such an emotional impact. It was, he said, an experience he would never forget.

But home video is wonderful, too. It's a great medium for seeing a film when you can't afford to go to the theater, especially with the outrageous prices that are being charged at the box office these days. It's wonderful for keeping movies alive, for exposing new generations to the great films of cinematic history; for allowing you to savor a favorite movie or favorite actor's performance time and again; for studying the techniques of great directors, writers, cinematographers, and other crafts people; for a terrific evening at home with friends, and as an alternative to TV's mind-numbing sitcommery. And home video, being relatively immune to the box-office numbers, is often the only way to see wonderful little movies that slip on and off the screens when they can't cut it in the mass market, and to see foreign films as well.

End of sermon. Pass the offering plate. Let's now get down to business. And don't blame me if you don't see these mistakes—they may be lost in the translation from film to TV, even from one TV set to another.

Boom Times

When Anjelica Huston and John Cusack are talking in the living room of his apartment in *The Grifters* (1990), the mike boom dips into the scene. The shadow of the mike also falls across Scarlett O'Hara's dress in a scene from *Gone With the Wind* (1939).

One reader reported that when he saw *Friday the 13th, Part VI: Jason Lives* (1986), the boom mike came into the picture so often that people in the theater were booing it.

The boom mike can be seen reflected in the shiny top of a jukebox when John Travolta and Olivia Newton-John meet at the malt shop in *Grease* (1978). And it cruises across the top of the screen as Warren Beatty comes down a staircase in *Heaven Can Wait* (1978).

In the classic *North by Northwest* (1959), watch for the microphone looming over Cary Grant and Eva Marie Saint during a conversation in the Chicago train station. It also makes frequent appearances in *Executive Action* (1973), especially in the scenes with Will Geer.

A microphone comes into frame in the wedding scene in *The Ruling Class* (1972) and literally hangs around for the rest of the ceremony. And a dramatic shot in *The Trip to Bountiful,* (1985), when Geraldine Page is standing in the middle of a cornfield, is spoiled when the microphone pops into view.

A variation on the meandering mike theme occurs in *The Big Chill* (1983) when Kevin Kline is wearing a body microphone, which you can see when his sweatshirt clings to his body. He should be glad that he didn't share the experience of Leslie Nielsen, who wears his RF mike to the john in *Naked Gun* (1988), or that of the actor, who shall go nameless (because the sound man wouldn't tell us), who forgot that he was wearing a live, switched-on RF mike when he went back to the trailer for a "quickie" during a break. The crew was, of course, gloriously entertained.

Mike's Still Pesky

Not even comedian John Candy's bulk nor comely Daryl Hannah's charms can detract from the obvious mike that's intruding on more than one scene in *Splash* (1984) ... and there's even one following Dennis Quaid around in a scene in *Suspect* (1987) where he has a lengthy discourse with an older woman.

Independence Day

Hold on tight! Earth is spinning out of control in *Independence Day* (1996). When you see our planet in the shot of the alien mother ship at the beginning, it's spinning at about two or three degrees per second. Let's see…that would make our days about two or three minutes each.

A seminal moment is the destruction of the Empire State Building, which the movie erroneously places in the middle of a main street. It blows up twice, each time differently.

Another location error comes in the map of Russia we see during the Russian broadcast of "Sky News." It shows the city of Petrograd. That was the city's name from 1914 until 1921, when it became Leningrad. In 1991 it was restored to its original name of St. Petersburg.

When President Whitmore (Bill Pullman) comes down the stairs, he hands a copy of *USA Today* to a staffer. You can see the weather map on the back page, showing temperatures in the 40s well into the south. Seems like things are colder than they should be. It's the Fourth of July, after all, and the next scene shows David (Jeff Goldblum) and Julius (Judd Hirsch) playing chess in Central Park as a radio reporter says that the high in New York is 95 degrees.

Watch how the Stealth bomber fires the nuclear missile at an alien ship, then banks to its left. On the satellite map it is seen to be turning to its right.

When David (Jeff Goldblum) and Constance (Margaret Colin) are in Area 51, Jeff reaches into the refrigerator to get some ice, and we see food stored in the rack on the inside of the door. But when they argue and Constance opens the door to put a drink back into it, the food has disappeared. And speaking of Area 51, there's a lot of secrecy about it, but it's nowhere near Death Valley, as shown on the radar map in the command bunker.

We also noticed that the Commander of the Black Night Squadron apparently received a field demotion. During the initial briefing, he's wearing a lieutenant colonel's oak leaf cluster. During the attack at the base he's wearing captain's bars.

Military types also noticed a slew of errors involving aircraft, procedures, and the like—something you'd probably have to expect in a sci-fi epic such as *Independence Day*. One flub-spotter observed pilots making high-speed turns without flight suits, which would cause them to black out and lose control. The all-powerful President Whitmore (Bill Pullman) shoots missile three from his plane ("Eagle 1, Fox 3"), but when he fires for the second time, it's Fox 3 again. When did he land for a reload? But it's only a movie.

FUZZY LOGIC

There are times when things you see on film just don't make sense. More often than not, under the pressure of production deadlines or in the midst of the the controlled chaos of a film set, writers or directors make certain assumptions, or just don't think things out. They think a radio works a certain way, then write it into the script as a plot point. But in real life, the same device can't do what they thought it would. What seem to be the symptoms of one illness are really the symptoms of another. Or it's assumed that a particular college offers a certain degree, because most do. Then, when the film is out in the marketplace, they find that their assumption was off-base, or an alert moviegoer spots the instances when things just weren't thought out. Some examples of skewed logic:

Without a Trace

A reader who works in the pager industry was taken aback during a scene in *Eraser* (1996). When Kruger (Arnold Schwarzenegger) gives a pager to Lee Cullen (Vanessa L. Williams), the bad guys trace a call to the pager in Chinatown. While they might have gotten the pager number, there's no way to trace a pager's location. The signal doesn't go out from a single tower.

The Premise Is All Wet

A major plot point in *The Rainmaker* (1997), from the John Grisham novel of the same title, involves an insurance company claiming bankruptcy to avoid paying a judgement. However, a New York lawyer who specializes in bankruptcy cases points out that under federal law an insurance company cannot file for bankruptcy protection. Insurors are covered by state law, which usually requires an insolvent company to go into receivership. Maybe this is a case for Wayne Emmons, who plays Prince Thomas in the film and was also its legal advisor. Emmons is well known in Memphis as the attorney for several topless bars.

Don't Sweat It

Some medical types noticed that when diabetic Baby-O (Mykelti Williamson) is deprived of his insulin in *Con Air* (1997), he breaks out in a cold sweat and nearly dies. However, the symptoms he exhibits are those of *too much* insulin. In the case of too little insulin, there would be symptoms such as lethargy and excessive urination, but not sudden collapse.

So Who Moved Our Trees to Costa Rica?

In a scene from *Jurassic Park: The Lost World* (1997) set in a Costa Rican rain forest, we see giant redwood trees. So what's the problem? Well, giant redwoods grow only in three places in the world: Northern California, a section of the Sierra Nevadas, and in a remote province of China. (The scene was shot near Eureka, California.)

It Just Doesn't Work That Way

The scripters of *Con Air* (1997) didn't really understand how a transponder works when they wrote the part where one transponder is transferred to another airplane to avoid radar detection. A transponder doesn't send out a code specific to the instrument itself. It echoes back a code that the ground controllers tell the pilot to dial into it *after* takeoff, which identifies the plane on radar. So the transponder would have to be changed from one plane to another in midair for the gambit to work.

19

No Magna Cum Laude for the Writers

Sometimes it's the smallest things that slip by scriptwriters. Since the late Carl Sagan is no longer around to defend himself, we wonder if the other writers of *Contact* (1997) knew that Dr. Eleanor Arroway (Jodie Foster) could not have graduated Magna Cum Laude from the Massachusetts Institute of Technology, since we're told that MIT doesn't offer such distinctions with its degrees. Notice also that at the White House press conference Ellie's badge is white with an outline of the letter "T." Later, at the same press conference, it's blue with a solid white "T."

The Script Sprang a Leak

An eighteen-wheeler driver noticed that in *The Long Kiss Goodnight* (1996) brake fluid is leaking as Geena Davis is driving an eighteen-wheel tractor trailer. He was a bit taken aback, since the big rigs all have air brakes; they don't use brake fluid. Also they have a "fail-safe" brake system. If a line is cut, the brakes lock automatically. Note also the car roof, which comes off near the end of the film, then is miraculously repaired.

Wild About the Camera Plane

In *Wild America* (1997), there is a shot of Marshall Stouffer (Jonathan Taylor Thomas) flying in an open-cockpit airplane. The yellow wedge you see at the bottom of the screen is the tail of the camera plane. Among other goofs in the film, you have to wonder why they're invading the cave of sleeping bears in late summer. We don't think bears hibernate in August. Here's another one someone told us about. Take notes. We can't endure checking the movie again to verify it. Here's the story: Mark (Devon Sawa) has a green toothbrush, Marty (Scott Bairstow) a yellow one, Marshall (Taylor Thomas) a blue one. Marshall plots revenge against his brothers by washing the green and yellow ones in the toilet and putting them back in their cups. He snickers about his revenge while he and his brothers are brushing their teeth. But Mark is brushing with a blue brush, Marty with a green one, Marshall with the yellow. Did he outsmart himself and brush with the very one that he dipped in the john? It's your call.

Roses Aren't Forever

When President Shepherd (Michael Douglas) tries to charm Sydney (Annette Benning) with roses in *The American President* (1995), he mentions that they came from the White House Rose Garden. However, the couple is on their way to the State of the Union Address, which usually takes place in January, a pretty cold time in Washington. If any roses were growing at the White House at that time of year, they'd probably freeze their little buds off.

Twister

The 1996 hit *Twister* spun around on a whirlwind of flubs, earning that year's Flubbie Award as the "Flubbed-Up Movie of the Year." Perhaps the most noticeable of the slipups was the scene when Bill (Bill Paxton) and Jo (Helen Hunt) are hit by a flying grain combine while they're in the film's signature red pickup. An arm of the combine smashes the truck's windshield, but moments later when they barrel through an overturned house, the windshield is flawless—miraculously healed.

The truck also has a rather wonderful odometer. In an early shot of the dashboard, we see that the mileage is 000902. After they drive for a while, the mileage is 000239; that's 663 less! It's a used-truck dealer's dream. Notice also that no matter how much twisting, tossing, and trauma that the truck endures, the binoculars stashed on the dashboard never move. Are they welded in place?

One of *Twister*'s most memorable shots is the "twin funnel" scene, when Bill, Jo, and Melissa (Jamie Gertz) are driving on a one-lane dirt road across a lake. Just after a cow flies over

the truck, they cut to a shot from inside the cab. Glance out the back window and you'll see a car pass by on the opposite side of a four-lane highway.

Technical types also got a kick out of seeing Melissa make a panicked call on her cellular telephone as a twister bears down on them. Odds are pretty high that the phone wouldn't work during such a storm.

Watch Bill's shirt when he comes down from taking a shower to have dinner at Aunt Meg's house. It is variously buttoned up and down throughout the meal.

WHEN THINGS GET HAIRY

Actors, being human (well, most of them), grow hair—or, in some cases, lose it. And when the filming of a movie stretches over weeks and months, stylists have to play close attention to hair length, lest it get away from them and cause a bit of cinematic weirdness. (Generally a film would be shot in reverse sequence so that an actor with long hair or a beard could have it shortened rather than having to wait until it grows.)

Close Shave

John Wayne looks like a spry young whippersnapper brandishing a cavalry sword as he leads his troops into battle in the ads for John Ford's *Rio Grande* in 1950. The Duke's clean shaven, whether thwarting Apache uprisings or elsewhere romancing Maureen O'Hara. In the film itself, however, he's kind of world-weary and throughout sports a bushy mustache and a small goatee. Same can be said of his earlier *She Wore a Yellow Ribbon*—but scratch the goatee.

The Wet Look

Mandy Patinkin's wet hair changes shape from shot to shot in a scene from *The Princess Bride* (1987).

The Hair of Oz

It happened in *The Wizard of Oz* (1939). Judy Garland's hair changes length at least three times during the course of the film. When Dorothy is brought to the Wicked Witch's castle, her hair is mid-length. When Toto runs away, the tresses are down to her belt; and when the witch turns the hourglass, Dorothy's hair is up to her shoulders.

10/31/38
Original Dress
own Hair & fall
before darkening

Duking It Out

In his classic *North to Alaska* (1960), John Wayne loses his hairpiece during a fight scene...but in the next shot, the rug's right back on again.

Godzilla

Filmmakers Roland Emmerich and Dean Devlin shoulda known better. When you try to remake a camp-cult classic such as *Godzilla,* you're treading into waters populated by fans who know every frame and sprocket hole of the series, and can tell you everything from the relative size of the monster to the way the crew demolished model buildings in the old films (they did it with a stick that you can see in some of them).

Newspaper writers went on mightily about inconsistencies. Marshall Fine, writing in the *Los Angeles Times,* pointed out that among the many questions raised were how Manhattan was evacuated in about fifteen minutes flat, while it took two hours to evacuate the World Trade Center after the (real) 1993 bombing. And if Godzilla is supposed to be twenty stories tall, how did he squeeze into Madison Square Garden to lay those eggs?

Who recorded the videotape that the French sent to the American military when secret service agent Jean Reno questioned the sole survivor of Godzilla's fishing boat attack?

Neither Reno, his assistant, nor the fisherman had a camera. Was it a survelliance tape?

The filmmakers obviously were having their revenge against critics Gene Siskel and Roger Ebert with Michael Lerner's Mayor Ebert and his assistant Gene (Lorry Golden.) After all, the critics weren't too kind to *Independence Day*.

An Internet Web site delivered even more inconsistencies. For example: How was the fish in the basketball hoop still alive after being out of the ocean for at least a day (and how did Godzilla carry all those fish to leave a trail, anyhow)?

Another interesting observation relates to the strength of the Brooklyn Bridge. Not only can it hold Godzilla, it can even hold him after it loses its suspension. So what are all those cables up there for, anyway?

The filmmakers missed a potent weapon against Godzilla— Fidel Castro. The monster walks across the Isthmus of Panama and walks across Jamaica. But he swims around Cuba. What was he afraid of?

And there are more. Many more. Find them for yourself. We're tired.

TIME TRAPS

It's one of the laws of nature that everything changes but change itself. But when it comes to a film, some things don't change, even when they should. Historical accuracy is one of the most daunting tasks of the filmmaker, and most put a real effort into making sure that all of the elements of their films are "of the period," and that they actually existed during the time the story is set. But little bugaboos slip in.

One of the surest ways to catch an anachronism is to look at flags. Over the years, most nations' flags have changed, often in very subtle ways. The American flag has changed many times, notably in the number and pattern of its stars. (Here's a hint: The current "staggered row" pattern of fifty stars in alternating rows of six and five was adopted in 1960; from 1912 to 1959 it had forty-eight stars in even rows; and from 1908 to 1912, forty-six stars in staggered rows. Check your encyclopedia for other eras.) But there have also been changes in Britain's Union Jack, Canada's maple leaf flag, and many others. Check these out for instances when Hollywood let time fly away:

Time and Money

Director Arthur Penn owned up to a goof in *Bonnie and Clyde* (1967) when *Time* Magazine pointed out that the cash used in one of the bank robberies was from the wrong era. Penn said in an interview, "It's true.

When we were shooting the first robbery scene, we didn't have the right bills. And I said, 'To hell with it. Let's just shoot it. Who's going to care?' Well, *Time* cared!"

A Rim Shot Ahead of Its Time

When Wally (Erik von Detten) recalls a basketball game back in the 1950s during the movie version of *Leave It to Beaver* (1997), the net has a collapsible rim. A sports fan reports that the collapsible rim wasn't invented until the early 1980s.

A Union Jack Before Its Time

Disney's animated *Pocahontas* (1995) had no shortage of historical errors. The film starts with a flag that would have been correct for the founding of Jamestown in 1607, but a few scenes later a flag appears with the red corner-to-corner Cross of St. Patrick, which was added to the flag when Ireland joined the United Kingdom in 1801. The animators also had a a bit of a problem with physics in a scene when Pocohantas and Flit see themselves in John Smith's helmet. Their images are enlarged, but actually the convex surface of the helmet would make the images smaller.

Plucking on an Anachronism

Bad enough that in *Sunset* (1988) Wyatt Earp (James Garner) leaves Los Angeles heading for Pasadena into a beautiful sunset. Pasadena is *east* of

L.A. But when he and Tom Mix (Bruce Willis) go to the very first Academy Awards ceremony, way back in the 1920s, they go into a bar where a musician is playing an Ovation guitar, a brand not produced until the 1970s.

Preparing for the Future of Rail Travel

When Coach Dale (Gene Hackman) and his basketball team enter through door H into the Butler University field house in the sleeper hit *Hoosiers* (1986), a man raises the roll-up door and you see the Amtrack logo. Two questions: Why is there an Amtrack logo in a basketball field house? And, even more important, since Amtrack didn't take over the nation's railroads until May 1, 1971, why does the logo appear in a scene set in 1951?

Taking the Heat—a Bit Too Soon

A young mobster quotes a line from the movie *White Heat*, saying "Top o' the world, Ma…just like the movies," in *Dillinger and Capone* (1995). Hmm…*Dillinger and Capone* takes place in the late 1930s; *White Heat* was released in 1949.

The Fact-Checkers Were Asleep

In *Sleepers* (1996) Michael (Brad Pitt) examines Father Bobby (Robert DeNiro) in court, asking about tickets that he bought for a basketball game. Father Bobby says that he bought them with his Mastercard. The scene was set in the early 1980s, and the credit card was still called Mastercharge.

Conveniences of War

Modern conveniences invaded *Gettysburg* (1993) in more than one instance. When Gen. Robert E. Lee (Martin Sheen) comes out of his headquarters, look for a clothes-dryer vent on the side of the building. When a Confederate soldier shakes hands with General Lee, he has a tan line on his arm from a wristwatch. The drum skins have a Remo logo a bit before its time, and that old aerial bugaboo, jet contrails, can be seen when Colonel Chamberlain (Jeff Daniels) is talking to a group of prisoners.

And Here's the $64,000 Question

Why does a theater marquee promote Fellini's *La Dolce Vita* in *Quiz Show* (1994)? The game-show scandal took place in 1958; Fellini's film was released in 1960.

Et What, Elizabeth?

It's one of the most majestic scenes in all filmdom, when Elizabeth Taylor, that noted Egyptian, enters Rome in a regal procession in the 1963 *Cleopatra*. On her way into town, she passes under a triumphal arch—one that wasn't built until after the real Cleo's death in 30 B.C.

A Crate With No State

The Sound of Music (1965) was also set in the 1930s. In the scene where Julie Andrews takes the children to the market, several gaffe-spotters have pointed out that there is a crate stamped "Jaffa Oranges—Product of Israel." The State of Israel was not founded until May 1948. However, the "pan and scan" appears to have eliminated this gaffe from the video version of the film when it moves in on a dropped tomato.

We Are Siamese, If You Please

So goes the lyric from *Lady and the Tramp*. But someone should have told the Spielberg/Lucas crowd that in 1936, the time in which their movie, *Raiders of the Lost Ark* (1981) was set, the country that we call Thailand was still Siam. Early in *Raiders*, Indy's route is traced by a small airplane flying over a map which identifies one of the countries as Thailand. Sorry, guys, Siam did not become Thailand until 1939.

Who Framed the Pasadena Freeway?

In *Who Framed Roger Rabbit* (1988), there is much conversation about the plot to tear down "Toontown" to build the world's first freeway—from Hollywood to Pasadena, California. *Roger Rabbit* is set in 1947. However, the Pasadena freeway was already in place, having been built in 1940.

Bye, Bye, the Fourth of July

Things looked pretty authentic when *Born on the Fourth of July* (1989) covered the 1968-69 era...but the song played in the background was Don McLean's "American Pie," which wasn't released until 1971.

Shall we continue? Here's an interesting situation—a "time tunnel" continuity gaffe in a film about time travel! At Mackinaw Island's Grand Hotel on June 27, 1912, in *Somewhere in Time* (1980), a guest hums and sings "You Made Me Love You." The song was copyrighted in 1913, the year that Al Jolson sang it in *The Honeymoon Express*.

And there's more. *Grease II* (1982) takes place in 1961. At the bowling alley, you can hear "Our Day Will Come" by Ruby and the Romantics playing in the background. The Ruby and the Romantics recording wasn't released until 1963.

The Time of Music

Getting music into its proper era can be a bedeviling problem—one that wasn't overcome in the 1953 movie *The Eddie Cantor Story*. It's 1904, and Cantor sings "Meet Me Tonight in Dreamland"—a song that was written in 1909.

It happened again in *Thoroughly Modern Millie* (1967), wherein one of the big production numbers is "Baby Face." *Millie* was set in 1922, four years before that song was written.

And in one of the two television movies in 1988 about Liberace, a flashback sequence had Lee playing piano in a 1934 Milwaukee dive while the chanteuse sang "The Man That Got Away"—which wasn't to be written for another 20 years!

Displaced Suburbs

Although *The 'Burbs* (1989) is set in middle America, in some of the shots one can see The Disney Channel's office building in the background. It was filmed on the back lot of Universal Studios, just across the San Fernando Valley from the Disney Channel's headquarters in Burbank, California.

Intolerable

In one of the greatest scenes of one of the greatest films of all time, one of D. W. Griffith's assistants is seen in a coat and tie as the Persians storm a wall in ancient Babylon in *Intolerance* (1916).

Frankly, Andrea...

Andrea McArdle, playing Judy Garland in the 1978 TV movie *Rainbow*, sings "Dear Mr. Gable" to the tune of "You Made Me Love You," serenading a photo of Clark Gable as Rhett Butler. However, the scene is based on a real-life incident that happened a year before the filming of *Gone With the Wind* (1939).

USA Yesterday

Although the Al Pacino *Scarface* (1983) is set in 1980, there is a shot in which a *USA Today* vending machine can be seen; the paper didn't begin publishing until 1982. In another scene, there's a shot of a billboard advertising a 1984 Corvette.

They Might Be Getting a Little Ripe by Now

Sharp-eyed Bart Andrews reports that there are more than a few continuity errors in the 1989 *Steel Magnolias*—among the more interesting of which is that Sally Fields' two teenage sons remain the same age throughout the picture, even though about three years transpire. They don't change hairstyles or clothes.

Hello…How's That Again?

Dolly Levi does her matchmaking work at the turn of the century in Barbra Streisand's 1969 *Hello, Dolly!* Some of Hollywood's most elaborate sets were built for the production—many of which still remain at the entrance to the 20th Century-Fox lot in West Los Angeles. But when *Dolly* was filmed and the sets were dressed, a wrecked but relatively modern automobile was left sitting by the railroad track.

The Drummer Stumbles

As if *The Cotton Club* (1984) wasn't plagued with enough problems, a musician noticed that the drum heads used in the movie are of modern synthetic materials—not the type used by drummers in the 1930s, the time in which the movie was set, when drum heads were natural skins. And while we're vamping, we should point out that Fred Astaire plays the drums in one scene with wire whisks in *Daddy Long Legs* (1955). In the next shot, he's using wooden drum sticks.

Judy and Larry and Perry

Richard Rodgers and Lorenz Hart come to Hollywood to score their first film in *Words and Music* (1948), laughingly referred to as their musical "biography." There, Judy Garland (as herself) joins Mickey Rooney (as Hart) singing "I Wish I Were in Love Again." Actually, the song was written not for a movie but for the 1937 Broadway musical, *Babes in Arms*, at which time Hart was about forty-two and Garland fifteen—they'd hardly have been show-biz buddies. And while we're on the subject of *Words and Music*, did anyone notice that Perry Como is cast as Eddie Anders, a fictional (?) buddy of Rodgers and Hart, and as Eddie sings a couple of their songs. However, at the all-star finale to the film, he is introduced as Perry Como to sing "With a Song in My Heart."

Far and Away Too Late

Today show film critic Gene Shalit points out in his review of *Far and Away* (1992) that Tom Cruise, Nicole Kidman, et al. arrive to join the Oklahoma Land Rush in 1892. Makes one wonder how they were able to stake a claim to any Oklahoma real estate, since the Land Rush took place three years earlier, in 1889.

An Inoculation to Keep the Beasts Away

Just as did Kirk Douglas in *Spartacus* (1960), Marc Singer follows suit in *The Beastmaster* (1982). Even though both movies are set in ancient times, both actors sport rather prominent vaccination scars.

Messing Around With Otis Redding

Otis Redding's songs are so popular that they're heard in all sorts of movies—and now and again, they slip time frames. In *Dirty Dancing* (1987), which takes place in 1963, you hear Redding's "Love Man," which wasn't released until after his death in 1967.

In *Top Gun* (1986), we hear that Tom Cruise's father was a fighter pilot who disappeared in 1965 or 1966. Yet in a later scene, Cruise tells Kelly McGillis that both of his parents loved "Sitting on the Dock of the Bay" by Otis Redding. The song was released in 1968.

Not So Young and Gay

The word "gay" is heard all through *Victor/Victoria* (1982). The film takes place in the 1930s and "gay," as a pseudonym for homosexual, hadn't yet come into common use.

Who's Watching the Store?

In the movie *Three Little Words* (1950), a poster for the Marx Brothers 1928 Broadway show *Animal Crackers* uses a publicity still from MGM's *The Big Store* (1941).

Another Shorts Story

The prehistoric man that is thawed back to life in *Return of the Ape Man* (1944) is wearing cotton underwear beneath his animal skin loincloth.

Power Failure

In 1935's *Great Impersonation*, Edmund Lowe is seen going to bed by candlelight in an old English country house. But when he is awakened during the night, there's an electric light switch nearby.

Heaven Couldn't Wait

The British *Quadrophenia*, which marked Sting's acting debut, was filmed in 1979 with the action taking place in 1964. Look for the movie house playing Warren Beatty's *Heaven Can Wait*, which was released in 1978.

The Addams Family

In the evolutionary process from cartoon to cult-favorite TV series to big-screen movie, it's a shame that *The Addams Family* lost its *raison d'être*. It just wasn't funny. But enough people liked it to turn it into a hit, thus opening the doors to us for a few hits at its flubs.

Speaking of doors, that's where we first turn our attention. Notice that there are two "ejection chute" doors on the side of the house. At first viewing, the door on the left bears Pugsley's name, the one on the right Wednesday's. That's the way we see them when Uncle Fester is expelled. A little later, Wednesday escapes via her door, but this time it's on the left. Then, a few minutes later, when the family searches for her, the names are back in their original positions.

In one sequence, Gomez pulls the chain that sends Uncle Fester and him down the corkscrew slide to the lower vaults. As they slide they change places a couple of times, even though it seems too narrow for them to switch.

Note also that Margaret has some problems with the finger trap. First, she wears it, then is seen not wearing it—indicating that she must have known how to take it off. Then she puts it back on, but can't get it off until Morticia shows her how the next day.

Outside a motel, Lurch drinks some "lemonade" which makes him blow fire out of his mouth—burning the paint off a nearby wooden Indian and leaving it blackened, but in the next scene, it has been wondrously healed, paint and all.

At the party near the end of the film, Gomez juggles some rather dangerous objects. When the camera is on his face—and not showing the juggling—he smiles broadly as though he's having a very good time. Yet in the angled overhead shot, you see a very stern stunt double concentrating very hard on his performance.

SHOT TO SHOT...OR NOT

When things get broken, they aren't supposed to be fixed as quickly as they seem to be on film. Time after time, dented cars are mysteriously healed (in an earlier book we called it "the laying on of hands by Earl Scheib"). Glass that is broken in one shot is intact in the next. Inanimate objects, a.k.a. props, move from shot to shot without human or spiritual intervention. Things fall down, then are miraculously restored to their previous positions.

These are the "mismatches," the flubs that happen when things go wrong from one shot to the next. The simplest of all are the ones where an actor may have an arm up in one shot, down in the next. Most of these are caught in the editing process and fixed with an "intercut," a shot that goes between the other two to take your eye away from the sudden jumpy movement. Some involve a sunny sky turning cloudy in the next shot; others defy explanation.

Find some fun with these sequential slip-ups:

Topless No More

Carol (Helen Hunt), Melvin (Jack Nicholson), and Simon (Greg Kinnear), on their trip to visit Simon's family, breeze down the highway with the top down on the convertible Carol is driving in *As Good as It Gets* (1997). But when they pull to the side of the road, the top is up.

It Isn't a Strip Bar

Johnny C. (Robert Pastorelli) takes off his vest when Arnold Schwarzenegger asks him for help in the gay bar scene in *Eraser* (1996). There's a cutaway, then he's taking it off again.

A Moveable Feast

Near the opening of *Good Will Hunting* (1997), the math students are trying to understand some difficult concepts as Professor Lambeau (Stellen Skarsgård) lectures. The task might be made easier if the moveable chalkboard would stay in one place. It moves all over the wall from shot to shot. And while we're at it, some math scholars have pointed out that the combinatorial problems and solutions seen on blackboards in the movie are elementary ones, not the sort that would occupy a scholar of that professor's status (a Fields medalist) for years.

An Unclear Vision

When Ossie Davis falls down in the park in *I'm Not Rappaport* (1996), his eyeglasses do some pretty nifty tricks. First, they land face down on the sidewalk. Then when Walter Matthau gets to him, they're in a different position and partly open, pointing away from him. Then, in a later shot, they're pointing in yet another direction.

Keeping One's Antenna Up

When the gal pals attend the dance in *Romy and Michele's High School Reunion* (1997), Romy (Mira Sorvino) is hit by a limousine. As she rolls over it, the "boomerang" TV antenna breaks off of the back of the limo and lands beside her in the street. In a later scene the limo rolls into the dance without the antenna, but emerges with it back in place.

One More Thing to Blame on El Niño

Except for the most recent assault of El Niño, we don't get much rain in Los Angeles. Perhaps that's why there were several rain flubs in *L.A. Confidential* (1997). It's raining when Bud White (Russell Crowe) leaves Lynn Bracken's (Kim Basinger) house and it's still raining when he fights with Ed Exley (Guy Pearce) in the records room. Yet when they confront the District Attorney, it's clear and dry outside with no evidence of it having rained. Also, when White is at the motel and sees the pictures in the trunk of the car the ground is muddy from the pouring rain. But when the car drives away, it kicks up a cloud of dust.

The Mirror Breaks (Not)

Roy (Woody Harrelson) breaks both a mirror and door handle on his car with his hook in *Kingpin* (1996). A few scenes later, the mirror and door handle are back in place. In the same film, in a scene set in 1979, he uses a Brunswick Rhino bowling ball, which wasn't introduced until 1987, and a mailbox sports a Postal Service logo that wasn't in use in 1979.

Unhappy With Happy

The director could not have been too happy with the continuity of *Happy Gilmore* (1996). When Happy (Adam Sandler) is trying out for the hockey team, he shoots a puck into the sideboard plexiglass and shatters it. Then we see the coaches standing behind the same glass—and it's fine! And that's not the only goof in this movie. A car can be seen crashed into the TV tower *before* the incident that caused the crash takes place, and in a really sad goof, his grandma's purse disappears from under her bed in the nursing home.

"For Never Was a Story of More Woe, Than Juliet and Her Romeo"

So says Shakespeare, and he might well have been speaking of the flubs that happened in the most recent rendition of his tale of the star-crossed lovers. Poor Romeo (Leonardo DiCaprio) and Juliet (Claire Danes) get so worked up at the end of *Romeo and Juliet* (1996) that a whole series of continuity problems emerge. After Juliet takes the poison, her left hand changes from being above the cover to below it. The vial of poison falls from his hand when she touches his cheek, but later she takes it out of his hand. And notice that when Juliet reaches for his gun, his shirt is open and unbuttoned. But after she kills herself and we see the bodies, his shirt is closed and buttoned up again.

Things Are a Bit Off in Face/Off

There are a few glitches in the transformation of Castor Troy (Nicolas Cage) and Sean Archer (John Travolta) in *Face/Off* (1997). Even though the faces and some other characteristics are switched, Troy seems to gain quite a bit of hair on his knuckles when he's wearing Archer's face. And even though Archer makes a point of his wife's being a vegetarian when telling of their first date, she doesn't question the nonvegetarian food, including lobster, provided by Troy when he's impersonating her husband.

Dad's a Turkey, Too

Wayward father Ed Munn (John Goodman) staggers in drunk, carrying a turkey and making a fool of himself in *Stella* (1996) during a scene when Stella (Bette Midler) allows their daughter to spend the holidays with him.

Moments later he storms out, and as he slams the door a wreath falls from it. Then, in the same scene, when Stephen (Stephen Collins) and Jenny (Trini Alvarado) leave, the wreath is back in place on the door.

It's There When You Need It

Never doubt the power of a Godfather. There's no glass on the table near Senator Geary (G. D. Spradlin) when he's talking to Michael (Al Pacino) in *The Godfather, Part II* (1974). But when he decides it's time to take a pill, a glass of water is right on the table waiting for him.

The Automatic Door Opener

Things get a little loopy when Lieutenant Kaffee (Tom Cruise) gets looped in *A Few Good Men* (1992). He staggers in and leaves the door open. Lieutenant Weinberg (Kevin Pollak) closes it, but a few moments later, when Weinberg and Lieutenant Commander Galloway (Demi Moore) get ready to leave, it's open again.

Lids Lost and Found

When a wagon goes off a cliff in *City Slickers II: The Legend of Curly's Gold* (1994), the lid from a water cooler flies off, spraying water into the air. In the next shot of the falling wagon, the lid is securely in place.

Somebody Touched It

A dead body moves from one part of the room to another in *The Untouchables* (1987), even though nobody touches it.

Changing Places

Look for a bottle of beer to move from the towel dispenser on the left to the one on the right during a restroom visit from "brothers" Danny De-Vito and Arnold Schwarzenegger in *Twins* (1988).

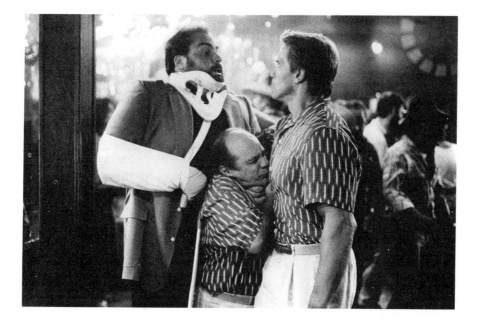

A Sack Full of Trouble

Bill Murray decides to go AWOL in *Stripes* (1981), but buddy Harold Ramis catches up with him and wrestles him to the ground. From one camera angle, Murray's head rests on his duffle bag; from another, the bag is at his feet.

They Went Thataway

By most standards, *Lawrence of Arabia* (1962) is one of the greatest films ever made. But even T.E. Lawrence's desert epic isn't without a flaw. Guess who our fearless flaw-spotter is, in this instance? None other than the director himself, David Lean. Lean told an interviewer that when he was reconstructing the film for its 1989 re-release, he noticed that in one scene, camels went from left to right in the first reel, then right to left in the second. Then he noticed that Peter O'Toole's wristwatch was on the wrong arm in the second reel. "It turns out that they'd flopped an entire reel," Lean told an interviewer. "They'd flopped the whole damn thing."

The error apparently happened when the 35mm print was struck in 1966. All of the theatrical, video and TV prints of *Lawrence of Arabia* since that time contain ten minutes of film with reversed images—a gaffe that has now been corrected.

Shadowing the Stars

As Scarlett and Melanie minister to the wounded in a sequence in *Gone With the Wind*, the shadows of the two dedicated ladies don't match their movements.

In *Miracle on 34th Street* (1947), on the other hand, a camera shadow follows Edmund Gwenn and John Payne as they walk across a square.

Son of Film Flubs

While taking a train trip in *Son of Frankenstein* (1938), Basil Rathbone calls attention to the weirdly stunted trees. One of the trees manages to pass by the train window three times. Incidentally, this was Boris Karloff's last film as the Frankenstein monster. Was he felled by the trees?

Grounds for Burial

In Stephen King's *Pet Sematary* (1989), Dale Midkiff, playing Dr. Louis Creed, sits next to his son's grave. A bouquet of purple flowers adorns the one to his right. After a cutaway to a recurring zombie apparition, the camera returns to Creed, and the purple flowers are now yellow. Also, the once-hazy sky has miraculously and instantly cleared.

Georgia on Your Mind

Next time you revel in *Gone With the Wind,* scan the scene at the famous Battle of Atlanta panorama. See if you can tell which of the wounded laid out at the railway station are live actors, and which are dummies. You might as well know, too, that as Scarlett runs through the streets from Atlanta, she passes an electric light. Isn't it interesting that progressive Atlanta had electric lights in the Civil War era, while all those other cities were having to use gas light? Frankly, Scarlett ...

Numbers, Please

Director Lloyd Bacon mixed actual game footage with his own scenes to create the football sequences in *Knute Rockne—All American* (1940). A very effective approach—except in the game footage the players had uniform numbers, and in the close-ups they didn't.

But Officer, You Must Be Mistaken

A motorcycle policeman stops Lily Tomlin in *9 to 5* (1980) because she is driving a car with one taillight out and the other blinking. But when she drives away, both lights are working just fine.

The Doorway to Weight Loss

Walter Matthau had a heart attack during the filming of *The Fortune Cookie* (1966). It was five months later before he came back to finish the scene that was being shot earlier, so this time he came through the door forty pounds lighter!

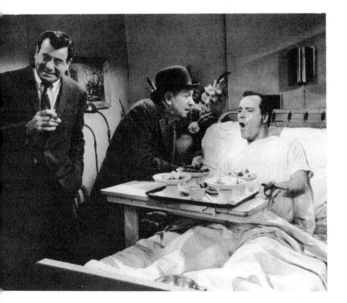

A Reversal of Recollections

Again we have a report straight from the set...this time involving a scene in *Reversal of Fortune* (1990). Our reporter, who shall remain nameless for obvious reasons, saw a flub abornin' as a scene was being shot. But, on-set politics being what they are, he was in a lowly position where pointing it out could have been problematic, so he kept his mouth shut, and the gaffe went into continuity history.

Ron Silver and Annabella Scioria create contrasting flashbacks to compare Alan Dershowitz's theory with lady friend Sarah's. In her version, when Sunny von Bülow (Glenn Close) is dragged into the bathroom, a window is opened, providing evidence against husband Claus. While the Dershowitz version was being shot, someone forgot to open the window, actually changing the evidence and insinuating that he (Claus) did try to kill her. Our informant told the script supervisor about the error the next day and pointed out that the closed window was not part of the script, but was told it was too late to change it. So it's there on the screen, actually confusing the story. In fact, the bedroom window is also closed in one version, and von Bülow opens it in the differing version. So we're really confused by the whole business. You'll have to figure it out for yourself.

The Cagney Haymaker

James Cagney gives it to Robert Armstrong on the chin in *G-Men* (1935). But when Armstrong gets up from the floor, he has a black eye.

The Growing Bandage

After Kevin Kline cuts his finger while slicing a tomato in *Grand Canyon* (1991), his wife bandages it, covering about an inch of his finger. Then an earthquake hits, and they run outside. Barely a split second transpires, but the bandage now covers his entire finger.

Bogie Gets Familiar

Oh, no...we're on Bogie's case again. In *The Maltese Falcon* (1941), Sam Spade (Humphrey Bogart) is seated in a chair in front of Brigid (Mary Astor), who's sitting on a sofa. He leans forward to make a point—and in the next shot, he's on the sofa beside her.

The Rock

Slam-bang action movies such as *The Rock* (1996) seem to be prone to more flubs than the calmer, "people" movies. Perhaps it's just impossible to keep track of everything because so much is going on and so many first, second, and third units are working on the film.

Whatever the reason, it seems that someone should have noticed that when Goodspeed (Nicolas Cage) chases Mason (Sean Connery) in a yellow Ferrari, the windshield breaks during the chase, but is intact when the car crashes into the parking meters. Same thing happens to the Humvee. Its windshield repairs itself after the crash through the water truck. When the Humvee crashes into the parking enforcement vehicle, it skids and veers sideways. But in the next shot, it has turned and is pointed straight down the street.

The Navy SEAL helicopters do a fast turn-around. As they approach the drop zone, mission control says that their heading is "bearing 275." That's nearly due west in aviation terminology. Then they're said to be heading "due east for Alcatraz."

Another directional problem comes when the FBI says that the first rocket is headed for Oakland, but it seems to be headed for Candlestick Park, on the opposite side of the bay.

While we're speaking of the armed services, the planes that drop the plasma are Navy F-18s. But they have Air Force markings. Even more interesting is that the plane which rolls out of the hanger is a two-seater, but all the aircraft in the squadron are single-seaters.

Notice also that when Mason and Goodspeed look through an opening in a wall, it's open when Goodspeed looks at it, but closed when he motions for Mason to look.

Conspiracy buffs noticed that Mason is imprisoned in Alcatraz in 1962 for stealing files about the Kennedy assassination, which was, of course, in November of 1963. However, others contend that it's a plot point proposing that in 1962 the government had confidential documents about an upcoming presidential assassination. Hmm....

Champagne Flight

A bottle of champagne is sitting upright in a bucket when Ron Richardson (Martin Mull) and Caroline Butler (Terri Garr) are in his plane in *Mr. Mom* (1983). But in the next shot, the bottle leans to one side, then is back upright in the third shot.

IN THE BALLPARK

There's no fan like a baseball fan. When studios start making movies about the national sport, they'd better watch their p's and q's and RBI's. The fanatic fans can spot any little glitch and it can drive them crazy. After all, when you're dealing with people who can quote stats back to Ty Cobb, do you think that they'd let a director get away with even the smallest baseball flub?

Flubdom seems to move from one filmic generation to another. *The Babe Ruth Story* (1948) was replete with historical errors. We are told that in his last game, Ruth hit three home runs and one single; actually he went hitless in one at-bat in that particular game.

Yet another from the film is that in the scene where Babe (William Bendix) hits his 60th home run in 1927 and rounds the bases, you can see signs on the Yankee Stadium bleachers for Ballentine Beer and Calvert Whiskey. Pretty daring for the park's owners, don't you think, since Prohibition was still in effect (until 1933)?

Then after seeing *The Babe* (1992), critic Gene Shalit went to the history books when, during the climactic game of the movie, a pinch-runner was used for a home run. Not in that particular game, Shalit says. Besides, another fan says, it's an error to use a pinch-runner on a home run.

Baseball films have been Hollywood favorites over the years. When they're flawed, fans are quick to take pen in hand. Some reports:

The First Shall Be Last

In *The Natural* (1984), Roy Hobbs (Robert Redford) is playing for the New York Knights, and the announcer makes it abundantly clear that the team's up in the bottom half of each inning. Hobbs wins the game with a home run; but he's on the visiting team and should be playing in the top of the inning. The home team always bats last.

Doubling the Error

Much has been made of Ray Liotta's right-handed batting portrayal of southpaw Shoeless Joe Jackson in *Field of Dreams* (1989). But an alert fan also noticed that while Shoeless Joe batted left, he pitched right-handed; just the opposite of the way Liotta plays the part. Also, Jackson—that he has his index finger outside his glove. That's a practice that didn't come into being until the fifties or sixties, not in Shoeless Joe's era.

A Series of Reverses

Eight Men Out (1988) had left-handed hitter Eddie Collins played as a right-hander, while Dickie Kerr, who threw left-handed, was seen pitching right-handed. In addition, the players in the picture are seen with a forefinger sticking out of their gloves. They wouldn't have in 1919, when the scandal took place.

Tricky Dickey

The Pride of the Yankees (1942) provided *FILM FLUBS* readers with a delightful tale about Gary Cooper's problems in batting left-handed and an editor's ingenious solution. Now there's more. In the film, Cooper, playing Lou Gehrig, looks in awe at the names of famous players on their lockers when he arrives in 1923. One of the names is Bill Dickey, later to become one of Gehrig's closest friends. But Dickey didn't join the Yankees until 1928. He also sees the names of Tony Lazzeri and Mark Koenig, both of whom joined the team after Gehrig.

Ronnie Could Always Count on His Wife

Ronald Reagan seems to have always had wives, real or cinematic, who could stretch the truth, when convenient. Take *The Winning Team* (1952), for example, when he played pitcher Grover Cleveland Alexander. In his rookie year, which would make it 1911, Doris Day, playing Mrs. Alexander, is talking with the other players' wives before a spring training game. Referring to the opposing pitcher, she says "That's Eddie Plank. He won twenty games last year." In 1910, Eddie Plank won sixteen.

Major League Miscues

Although its baseball sequences were set in Cleveland, Ohio, much of the 1989 *Major League* was filmed in Milwaukee, Wisconsin. Thus, even though the game is supposedly being played in Cleveland's stadium, we see the logo of Milwaukee station WTMJ over the scoreboard—which also features a Milwaukee Brewers logo.

And as if that wasn't enough, there are problems with the scoreboard clock—the same kind of gaffe that hearkens back to 1934 when time apparently stood still in the aforementioned *It Happened One Night.* In *Major League*, the clock reads 10:40 (presumably A.M., since the scene is played in sunlight—but then how many major league games are played in the morning?). However after a base hit, a conference on the mound, and a scene in the broadcast booth, there's a cut back to the clock—which still reads 10:40.

Later in the movie, the clock remains at 10:20 (P.M., we suppose, since it's dark outside) from the seventh inning on during a playoff game.

We May Have to Revoke Their Dramatic License

Hard-core fans had a field day comparing on-screen events with reality in *The Pride of the Yankees* (1942). In one scene, Gary Cooper, as Lou Gehrig, tries to awaken his future wife (Teresa Wright) in the middle of the night by throwing pebbles at her window. A cop walks by and asks what he is doing there, and he says he's going to ask her to marry him.

Just prior to that scene, Gehrig and his teammates are seen beating the St. Louis Cardinals. Historians noted the Yankees beat the Cardinals only once prior to 1943—in 1928 when they swept the series. Gehrig and girlfriend Eleanor married in 1933, meaning that he strolled around for about five years on the way to her house.

In a touching scene, Babe Ruth (played by Babe himself) and Lou Gehrig promise a sick young boy that they will both hit homers for him, in a conversation in the boy's room in St. Louis. That would make it 1926 or 1928, the only years during Gehrig's career when the Yankees played World Series games in St. Louis. In the movie, Babe Ruth hits one home run and Gehrig hits two. There was no game in which this actually happened.

The real truth is that producer Sam Goldwyn moved the "called" home run of the 1932 Series from Chicago to St. Louis. The actual incident happened on October 1, 1932, and Ruth did hit two homers that day. Gehrig's two home runs in a World Series game against St. Louis were in 1928.

Back to the Future

Granted, when you're dealing with a trilogy such as the *Back to the Future* movies (two of which were made back-to-back), there are more than enough possibilities for error. In the first place, there are time shifts within each movie, then there are time shifts back and forward to previous and future films. Add flashbacks and flash forwards to the mix—and the shooting of "II" and "III" at the same time, and you have the recipe for disaster. It's a tribute to director Robert Zemeckis, writer Bob Gale, and everyone else involved that they were able to keep their wits about them. But...there were a few slips, and flub-spotters caught them.

Let's see. In the original, Marty McFly (Michael J. Fox) goes into a diner in 1965, and pays for his coffee with change from his pocket. He should be glad that the cashier didn't look too closely at it, since it would be 1985 money.

There's a real time shift when Marty jumps into the DeLorean to escape the Libyan terrorists. The odometer

mileage is at first 33061 then it zaps back to 32904 a few seconds later. Sounds like what happened in *Smokey and the Bandit* (1977) where the mileage on Burt Reynolds Trans-Am never changes. Never buy a used car from a movie studio.

Fans of TV's *The Honeymooners* know their show so well that several caught a flub when Marty visits his *Back to the Future* mother-yet-to-be. It's November 5, 1955, yet they're watching an episode with Jackie Gleason and Art Carney entitled "The Man From Space." That episode first aired on December 31, 1955.

When Doc (Christopher Lloyd) is hanging from the clock near the end of the film, he's wearing sneakers with Velcro straps. Velcro wasn't invented until 1967, and didn't appear on shoes until a few years later.

Marty McFly writes a note to Doc about his future demise on dinner stationery. Doc tears up the note, but in the last scene, after he's been saved from a hail of gunfire by his bulletproof vest, he hands the taped-up note back to Marty. But the restored note is on different stationery.

When Marty does his guitar riff on the high school stage, the giant amplifier blows him into a bookshelf filled with paper, all of which falls on him. In the long shots, it's all on Marty. In the subsequent close-ups, more paper is seen falling.

And finally, we have to wonder if Texaco paid some bucks to join the mass of advertisers who bought on-screen "product placement" time in "II." Doc stuffs garbage into the DeLorean, signifying that in the future there's no need for gasoline. Yet later, in the future, we see a modern-looking Texaco station. Do they pump gas or garbage?

THE EYE OF THE BEHOLDER

Perhaps the flubs that are trickiest to spot are those which involve geography. More often than not, they're "eyes of the beholder" gaffes. If you live in or are very familiar with a certain area, you may notice a car heading off in the wrong direction to its destination (a couple of classics occur in the 1967 film, *The Graduate*. Not only does Dustin Hoffman head the wrong way on the Bay Bridge when he's going from Berkeley to San Francisco, a few scenes later when he's southbound, he drives through a tunnel which locals know is only on the northbound lane of the road.) Some are a bit more obvious. The shot of the Empire State Building in *Independence Day* (1996) shows it straddling a street. The former Pan Am Building does that; the Empire State Building doesn't.

Even though many of us who don't live in a particular area can't spot its geographic flubs, if you notice something being geographically awry in a film, it's a definite goof. Directors have to be aware that their films will be shown in hundreds of cities around the world, and the odds are very high that someone will go "huh?" when they see a car turn a corner and suddenly appear on a street miles away.

Take a global spin on these geographic gaffes:

Lost in New York

New Yorkers noticed that the geography was all askew in *Ransom* (1996). No less than the *New York Times* itself related one geographical "huh?" The paper pointed out that Gibson leaves his home at Eighty-eighth Street and Fifth Avenue, and heads for the bank. In-car images indicate a very long drive, but when he gets to his bank, it's at Nintieth Street and Madison Avenue, only about three blocks away. As if that wasn't enough, even though New Yorkers can suspend their disbelief pretty easily (it's often a requirement for survival in the city), the one thing they couldn't accept was the ready availability of a parking space right at the bank's door. Others noticed that there are no "Oakland" exits on New York highways, even though one is seen in the film. Did they make a fast dash to California's Bay Area?

Get Out of Town—The Wrong Way

Here's one that hits close to home, since your Flubmeister grew up in the environs where this flub happened. Interestingly, it was also noticed by a Chicago reader who had gone to school in Memphis, where *The Firm* (1993) was filmed. If Mitch and Abby McDeere (Tom Cruise and Jeanne Tripplehorn) are leaving Memphis and heading for Boston, why are they going south toward Mississippi? Logically they should have headed northeast toward Nashville.

Thou Shalt Not Bear False Witness

In *Raiders of the Lost Ark* (1981), Indiana Jones (Harrison Ford) tells the two government agents that Moses received the Ten Commandments on Mt. Ararat. Wrong, Indy. The Commandments were handed down on Mt. Sinai. Mt. Ararat is supposedly the resting place of Noah's Ark.

And a Flub Is Still a Flub

"An airport is an airport." That's what a spokesman for Castle Rock Entertainment told *People* magazine when that journal wondered why, in *City Slickers* (1991), Billy Crystal, supposedly being met by his family in New York, actually arrives at the Bradley Terminal at Los Angeles International (LAX). Many, many flub spotters wondered, too, even though one of the LAX direction signs in the background had been changed to read "New York Helicopter." The production was based in L.A., and Castle Rock wanted to avoid the expense of flying the actors to New York to film the brief scene, just as did the producers of *Big Business* (1988), as reported in *FILM FLUBS*.

Gonna Build Me a Mountain

In William Faulkner's novel as well as the movie of *The Reivers* (1969), the setting is in Northern Mississippi and in Memphis, both located in an area that's pretty flat, except for some low, rolling hills with no sign of a mountain anywhere on the horizon. But the horse race scene has as its backdrop a range of towering, rugged mountains. It was shot in California.

There's an inside joke in the film, too. William Faulkner, on whose story the film is based, named the whorehouse "Binford's" after Memphis' notorious movie censor, Lloyd T. Binford.

Perhaps We Could Call It San Franangeles

Then again, perhaps Hollywood is trying to prepare us for the scientific prediction that when The Big One hits, the tectonic plate slip is going to draw San Francisco and L.A. closer together. In *Predator II*, what is supposed to be a Los Angeles subway has cars marked "BART"...that being the acronym for the San Francisco's Bay Area Rapid Transit system.

The Lost Brigade

History buffs won't let *Glory* (1989) get away with its wrong-way march. As the 54th advances on Fort Wagner, the Atlantic Ocean is on their left, meaning that they attacked from the north. Wrong. In the actual battle, they advanced from south to north, so the ocean should be on their right.

GoodFellas

Here we go again, catching flubs in a film that many critics—and your humble Flubmeister—consider far and above the best film of 1990. Martin Scorcese's *GoodFellas* (1990) is a lesson in all that is good in filmmaking—a strong story, fine acting, seamless directing, great cinematography. Watch it once for the story, then go back and watch it again to study how a film should be made.

But once again, we have our work to do. We have to tell you that at the beginning of the movie, it's 1963, but the boys are sitting on the back of a 1965 Chevy Impala at the airport waiting to steal a truck. At the same airport, look for a Boeing 747 taking off in the background. The airplane wasn't in use in 1963.

A tricky flub is Ray Liotta's high-speed religious conversion. Ray (as Henry Hill) is at his girlfriend's apartment when Paul Sorvino and Robert DeNiro come to talk him into going home to his wife. Notice that the cross he's wearing on his neck changes to a Star of David, then back again. We should point out that it's a plot point that he's married to a

Jewish girl and wears both the cross and Star of David on the same chain. But in this shot-to-shot sequence, there's no reason for them to change places.

While a restaurateur complains that some of the good-fellas haven't been paying their bills, wiseguy Paul Sorvino must be getting a bit flustered. As he listens, there's a huge cigar sticking out of his mouth, but in the reverse angles it isn't there.

And finally, when Lorraine Bracco drives away in the scene where she's sure that DeNiro is going to have her "whacked," the fake license plate on the car in front of her (one of the orange and blue ones formerly used in New York) falls off, revealing the current New York red, white and blue plate.

Der Flubmeister is now in serious danger of being "whacked."

DISAPPEARING AREAS
OF RESPONSIBILITY

Life has its mysteries. Some things we just aren't supposed to understand. Like crop circles, some things seem to appear and disappear on film for no apparent reason. Props vanish. Bites pop back into sandwiches. Things drawn into animation cels somehow get undrawn.

The usual explanation is to blame it on the script supervisor, the person in charge of continuity. Since movies are sometimes shot out of sequence, it's usually up to the script supervisor to make sure that the things that were there yesterday are back today, or if they weren't there before they shouldn't be seen now.

The fact is that every worker on a film is responsible for its particular area. Prop people are supposed to make sure the props are back in the same place. Costumers ensure that a shirt worn a week ago matches the one the actor is wearing today. Set decorators check to see that pictures are back up on the wall, that furniture is in the same place it was the last time the set was used.

Some films are so complicated that it's a miracle things aren't more messed up than they are, and some flubs defy explanation. When the schedule calls for a move from one scene to another, the Polaroid cameras come out, and pictures are shot of almost everything, from a scrap of paper on the floor to the fake blood splatters on a costume.

Still, there are slipups, not all of which happen on the set. Sometimes the editor uses the wrong footage, a take that shows something that wasn't there before, or makes a cut for the sake of action and accidentally causes a building to blow up twice. Often, the cause is scheduling. Major stars are often incredibly busy, so all of their scenes are scheduled to be shot one after the other, even if the scenes appear at various points in the film. Thus, the scene that follows a shooting may be filmed before the shooting itself, and a bullet hole appears before the gun has been fired, then it disappears.

Keep a sharp eye out for these instances when filmmakers aren't keeping up with appearances (or disappearances):

Presidential Protection

We've all heard that the president's airplane has some pretty nifty secret devices to protect the chief executive. But the movie *Air Force One* (1997) apparently reveals some interesting new technology. The terrorists fire bullets through the door of the conference room where the presidential party is hiding. A few shots later, when you see the door from the inside, the holes are gone. Similarly, bullet holes in the wall of the toilet seen from the inside don't match the pattern of the holes shot through the door of the toilet from the outside.

Do Chess Men Heed the Call of Nature?

A table is covered with chess pieces as Ace Ventura (Jim Carrey) cavorts in a very proper drawing room in *Ace Ventura: When Nature Calls* (1995). Carrey's wild antics must have frightened the chess pieces, because they disappear entirely and the chessboard is bare the next time we see it.

If It Bothers You, Get Rid of It

John Favreau's telephone answering machine in *Swingers* (1996) is the source of many of the frustrations of his love life—so many that during one scene he checks the machine for messages, then makes a call during which the answering machine disappears from his desk.

The **Catch-22** *Hat Trick*

Hollywood is full of "Catch-22" situations, named after the crazy situations in the book and movie of the same name. You can't be in a movie unless you join the actor's union (SAG), and you can't join the union until you've been in a movie. You can't join the writer's union (WGA) until you've sold a script, but you can't sell a script to a union production unless you're a member of the WGA. A movie company won't look at your script unless you're represented by an agent. An agent isn't interested in representing you unless you've sold a script. So we must honor a flub in *Catch 22* (1970). The film itself is a movie about the craziness of war. One of our readers in Israel noticed a bit of craziness when Yossarian (Adam Arkin) jumps out of the window of the whorehouse to escape being scratched up. He isn't wearing his hat. In the next scene, he's wearing it as he walks down the street.

Water and Power

Tracker Lewis Gates (Tom Berenger) discovers the power of water pressure in *The Last of the Dogmen* (1995) when he and Sheriff Deegan (Kurtwood Smith) are blown out of a cave behind a waterfall into a raging torrent. Gates is handcuffed, but the cuffs vanish while he's in the water and he's able to save both himself and the sheriff.

So She Can Sew

The Russian princess makes some alterations to her clothing in the animated *Anastasia* (1997). Dimitri gives her a dress with lace around the bottom edge when they're on the ship, but when she wears it later there's no lace. When Anya (Anastasia), Dimitri, and Vladimir escape a runaway train, they leave their luggage as they jump off. But in the next scene they are sitting on it on the side of the road.

No Way to Treat a Cop

Here's one of the more sickening flubs we've personally witnessed: in *The Chase* (1994), Kristy Swanson tosses her cookies out of the car window during a chase scene, covering the windshield of the cop car behind her with vomit. For a couple of shots, the cops have to see through the space cleared by the windshield wipers. Then, for the rest of the chase (the cop car never stops), it's car-wash clean.

The Magical Chandelier

Mrs. Trunchbull (Pam Ferris) jumps and sends a chandelier crashing to the floor when she's searching for the title character of *Matilda* (1996). But when Matilda (Mara Wilson) runs up the stairs to safety, the chandelier is still hanging from the ceiling.

Good Will Painting

When Gerald (Stellen Skarsgård) and Sean (Robin Williams) argue in Sean's office, a picture of a boat that earlier was leaning on a window ledge is missing. When Will (Matt Damon) enters in mid-tiff, the picture has magically returned to the window. Incidentally, the picture was painted by the film's director, Gus Van Sant (no slouch of an artist, he). And here's one that Damon and Ben Affleck, being natives of the area, should have caught. The closing credits offer a tip of the hat to "The State of Massachusetts." True, it is a state—but it's called "The Commonwealth of Massachusetts."

Score One for the Clean-Up Crew

As Julia Roberts falls back after being hit by a door in *My Best Friend's Wedding* (1997), an ash from her cigarette lands in her hair. In the next shot she's still on the floor and hasn't moved, but the ash has disappeared.

Animated Annoyances

Assembling an animated film requires meticulous craftsmanship and planning. After all, twenty-four individual drawings ("cels") have to be hand-crafted for each second of the film. We're talking 1,440 drawings per minute.

Nonetheless, errors can creep in. In *Snow White*, there is supposedly a moment where missing cels cause a flicker. And recently, animation buff William Simpson discovered that in the masterful *The Little Mermaid* (1989), Ursula's lipstick tube vanishes from her hand the moment before she applies it; a thimble that Sebastian the Crab catches on his foot disappears, then reappears, then vanishes again; lemon slices disappear from Grimsby's dinner plate; and there are several instances of positioning errors in transitions from long shots to close-ups.

Immune to the Wounds

In a dramatic scene near the end of *Lethal Weapon II* (1989), Mel Gibson shoots the bad guy five or more times in the chest as he calls out a list of names. As the man approaches him, the wounds disappear.

Losing Blood All Over the Place

John Amos gets blood all over his mouth when he and Bruce Willis fight on the wing of the airplane in *Die Hard 2* (1990). But the blood just disappears. In another fight scene, Willis gets blood on the right side of his face—but when he's on the ground laughing, the blood is, again, gone. Suddenly it reappears when he's looking for his wife.

Feats of Legerdemain

Fred Astaire was always known for his style and savoir-faire. He took it to an extreme, however, in *The Barkleys of Broadway* (1949) when, as he puts his arms around Ginger Rogers as they're riding in a cab, a lit cigarette pops into his fingers. Perhaps it's making up for the lit pipe that he put into his overcoat pocket in *Swing Time* (1936).

They Call It Vanishing Cream, Don't They?

In *Green Card* (1990), Gerard Depardieu gets a dollop of cream on his nose. (Stop me before I make a comment about that nose.) When he then comes into the room and sits down to talk to Andie MacDowell, the cream has disappeared.

Thelma's Magical Margarita

While *Dick Tracy*'s "kid" (Charlie Korsmo) is having trouble with that glass of milk, the same thing happens in a less wholesome situation in *Thelma and Louise* (1991). In the country-western bar scene, while Geena Davis dances, Susan Sarandon finds the magical margarita. For most of the scene, when we see her from the front taking a drink, it's down about an inch. But in the shots over her shoulder, it's full to the brim.

Liver, When You're Near Me...

Maybe Kevin Costner just didn't have the gumption to take a big bite out of that buffalo liver in *Dances With Wolves* (1990). In the long shots, it looks rather large, but in the close-ups, it's not only smaller but of a different shape. Did the prop people create something a bit more palatable for Costner between shots?

Postdate the Check

The date on the payoff check in *The Verdict* (1982) isn't consistent with the rest of the dates in the film, which are shown on phone bills and the like. Producer David Brown told Wayne Norman of radio station WILI-AM in Willimantic, Conn., that the date may well have been the day that the scene was shot.

The World's Fastest Purse-Snatcher

Just before Teri Garr knocks on Dustin Hoffman's door in *Tootsie* (1982), Hoffman's purse is laying on a table. In the next shot, it's gone. Now, is that a fast purse-snatcher, or what?

Maybe the Same Crook Stole 'Em Both

After she leaves the nursing home and goes back to the Whistle Stop Cafe in *Fried Green Tomatoes* (1991), Jessica Tandy is seen sitting on her suitcase as she wonders who "stole" her house. She might also ponder who slipped in and then stole her suitcase. An alert flub-spotter noticed that neither she nor Kathy Bates seems to be carrying it when they go back to the car, nor is it still in the road.

A Deli-cate Matter

There are just all sorts of problems with Goldie Hawn's sandwich in *Foul Play* (1978). As she lunches on a park bench, the sandwich is whole, then half-eaten, then uneaten again, then half-eaten, then it has just one bite out of it, then it disappears completely.

A Moment of Freedom

When Nick Nolte springs Eddie Murphy out of jail in *48 HRS.* (1982), Murphy is handcuffed. Soon we see Murphy with one arm stretched over the seat back. Then he's handcuffed again.

The *Indiana Jones* Movies

The Indiana Jones movies—*Raiders of the Lost Ark* (1981), *Indiana Jones and the Temple of Doom* (1984), and *Indiana Jones and the Last Crusade* (1989)—offer many opportunities for flub-finding fun. Their being action-adventure films means that there's much going on and many opportunities to slip up. Into the fray:

In the beginning, Indy and a Mexican man are in a cave. Indy says, "Adios, Sapito." The character is "Saripo" in the credits and "Satipo" in the novel.

When Indy's enemy Beloq and a group of German soldiers escort the Ark to a place on the island to open it, Indy shows up with a missile launcher. Beloq says, "You give mercenaries a bad name." Then a fly gives Beloq a bad taste as it lands on his face, and appears to crawl into his mouth. Did he eat it? Wonder if it's the same live-action fly which appears in the "Dance of the Hours" scene in Disney's animated *Fantasia* (1940). Does it have a SAG card?

A special effect goes awry when Indy faces the hooded cobra. There's a brief flash of light which reflects on the glass partition that separates our hero from the deadly snake. Really. Just like the one that comes between Cary Grant and the leopard which he finds in the bathroom in *Bringing Up Baby* (1938).

In *Indiana Jones and the Last Crusade*, Indy arrives at his father's (Sean Connery) ransacked house and finds that Dad is missing. He picks up his father's mail, then puts it down. But when he opens Dad's diary, he's still holding the mail.

When Indy is beaten up in the rainstorm, blood is on one side of his mouth. He hangs his head, and when he looks up, the blood has moved to the other side. During the truck chase, scaffolding and boulders fall on its roof mangling the roof rack—but the rack's back again, miraculously repaired, when the Nazi crawls over the roof.

When Indy's in the library talking to the wealthy backer, watch as both the amount of champagne in the glass and the position of his arm jump around as the film editor cut from shot to shot.

Indy and his father ride in the German zeppelin *Hindenberg*. The scene takes place in 1938. The *Hindenberg* disaster was in 1937.

A bit of model-maker inaccuracy: Inside the tank, there's plenty of passage between the body and the turret. But when it goes over a cliff and is destroyed, the turret comes off, revealing a solid top and the peg which holds it on.

When Indy's in the library and sees the giant "X" on the floor, marking the burial site of the Knight of the Grail, notice how when he sees the "X" from the balcony, the floor changes color as he gets down; but, more importantly, the "X" fades and disappears as he begins breaking through the floor.

Finally, the powers of the "Cup of Christ" are revealed when Indy uses it to heal his father's wound. He empties the cup onto the wound, turning it upside down, but when his father looks into it, there's about an inch of water therein.

MIRROR IMAGES

Mirrors—or anything else that's reflective and shiny—can be among the most troublesome props on a set, close behind food, drink and cigarettes. Camera crews have to be extremely careful that they aren't seen in reflections from anything that's shiny. And mirrors aren't the only problem. Storefronts, with their wide expanses of glass, are a particular problem.

Take *Carmen Jones* (1954), for instance. The camera tracks along as Dorothy Dandridge strolls down a shop-filled street. The camera crew can be seen reflected in the store windows.

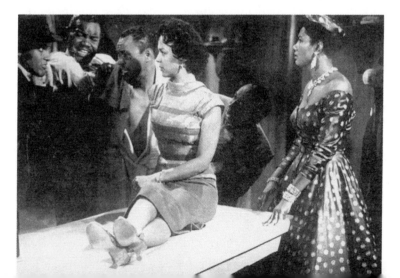

Similarly, in *A Christmas Carol* (1951), the camera crew can be seen in the mirror behind Alistair Sim in Dickensian London. And in the Meryl Streep/Robert De Niro *Falling in Love* (1984), you can see the reflection of the camera in a scene involving a mirror.

Then there are some other mirror problems on which you might wish to reflect:

Selective Reflections

It's a given in ghost lore that ghosts don't cast reflections. But in one scene in *Beetlejuice* (1988), even though you can't see the reflections of the ghosts (Geena Davis and Alec Baldwin) in the mirror, you can certainly see them reflected in a windowpane.

Monstrous Images

It's a basic tenet of vampire lore that the undead creatures don't cast reflections, right? Well, in the 1979 *Dracula*, when Dr. Von Helsing goes in search of a female vampire in an underground cavern, his first glimpse of her is a reflection in a pool of water. Hmmmm…

Monstrous Images II (the Sequel)

The camera crew can be seen reflected in the glass covering Jeff Gold-blum's pod in *The Fly* (1988).

And how often have you noticed that in practically every movie ever made that has its actors seated in a car, when a shot is made through the front windshield, there is no rearview mirror? It's generally been removed so as not to obstruct the actors' faces.

Awakenings

We hope the Marshall family won't be upset with us. We've said much about Garry Marshall's *Pretty Woman* (1990), now we're starting in on sister Penny Marshall's *Awakenings* (1990). But, like most Hollywood professionals, they're gracious about the flubs spotted in their films. Penny, in fact, event old an interviewer about a couple to look for. But we love you, Marshall. We really do.

But let us marshall our resources (sorry about that!). In *Awakenings,* when Dr. Sayer (Robin Williams) is testing the "frozen" Lucy (Alice Drummond) for her reflexes, notice the changing position of her eyes from shot to shot.

When the patients are listening to an opera recording, Dr. Sayer and nurse Eleanor Costello (Julie Kavner) watch them for reactions. The over-the-shoulder shot behind the three patients at the table shows quite a wind outside the open window, blowing the patients' hair. Yet when the camera does a full close-up on the woman in the middle, her hair is perfectly still.

In the scene where the awakened Leonard (Robert De Niro) is working on an architectural model with his mother (Ruth Nelson) seated next to him, he leaves to follow Paula (Penelope Ann Miller). When he looks back at his mother, there's a full paper bag on the seat which he just vacated.

A telephone company executive took note of the modular handset on Dr. Sayer's telephone. The film was set in 1969, when hard-wired connections were used. The modular connections came along in the mid-1970s.

And finally, the Marshalls do have problems with buttons. Near the close of the film, Dr. Sayer runs downstairs to meet Eleanor. His coat is buttoned in the long shots and open in the close-ups.

THINGS WHICH COUNT…OR DON'T

Perhaps the toughest flubs to catch are those which involve numbers. If you're really paying attention to the plot and action of a film, slipups involving numbers or things which should happen in a prescribed sequence just slide right through your consciousness and back out again.

But numerical and sequential situations offer a wealth of opportunities for screw-ups. Clocks can stay frozen for hours, or go forward and backward during a succession of scenes. Odometers can back up (without the help of a used car dealer!) Dates of events can be wrong, and we're always surprised when we hear that someone catches them. You gotta be really observant to catch that the day and date on a newspaper, driver's license, or even on a tombstone are out of kilter.

Count on spotting these instances when things just didn't count up:

A Low, Low Mileage Car

Jeff Taylor (Kurt Russell) drives a brand-new Jeep Cherokee through Arizona in *Breakdown* (1997). If they bought the Jeep in Boston and drove it cross country, why does the odometer read 000245 miles when wife Amy (Kathleen Quinlan) asks about his speed and then we see a shot of it?

Too High to Keep Count

Curly Bill (Powers Boothe) is a bit wacked out on opium in *Tombstone* (1993). Maybe that's why he pulls one of the oldest flubs in the book: he's carrying two six-shooters (we're talking twelve bullets if they're completely loaded), yet fires seventeen times without reloading. One alert viewer noticed that there's a pause when he could have reloaded, but on closer look saw that no bullets were missing from his ammo belt.

Delay of Game Penalty

Filmmakers do some fancy footwork with the date of Karen's (Jennifer Lopez) birthday in *Out of Sight* (1998). An early scene establishes that the date is but a week away from Super Bowl Sunday, which is usually in January. However, a shot of her license shows that her birthday is April twenty-fifth.

Where No Architect Has Gone Before

There are all sorts of architecture problems with the *Enterprise* in *Star Trek: First Contact* (1996). Lieutenant Commander Worf (Michael Dorn) is told that the enemy controls decks twenty-six to eleven during the Borg takeover of the ship A few minutes later, when asked how big the ship is, Captain Picard (Patrick Stewart) says "twenty-four decks." And when

Picard and Lily (Alfre Woodard) go into the holodeck they pass through a door marked "08 Holosuite 4." A few seconds later the Borg force open the same door, but now it's labeled "0820 Holodeck 02."

Looking Out for No. 1 (or was it No. 3?)

Given that John Travolta is, like your Flubmeister, a licensed pilot, you would think that he could have caught a some of the aeronautical flubs in *Face/Off* (1997). Several pilots noticed that when he fired at the Lockheed Jetstar, he destroyed the No. 1 engine. An airplane's engines are numbered starting from the pilot's left, but when the camera cuts to a shot of the inside of the cockpit it shows a fire warning light for Engine No. 3. Another shot shows a plane being taxied on the ground using the stick. It ain't done that way. Pilots steer the plane on the ground with their feet, using the stick only to compensate for wind direction. (By the way, Travolta, an aircraft collector, often uses his own personal jets in his films. Look for the initials JT on the plane's "N Number"—registration—on the tail.)

Monday's the Day for Funerals and Weddings

In *Roman Soldiers Don't Wear Watches*, we pointed out the error regarding Forrest Gump's wife's death date: he says "You died on a Saturday," but the date on the tombstone is a Monday. Well, it's happened again. An alert moviegoer noticed that in *The Wedding Singer* (1998) Drew Barrymore's wedding date is Sunday, August 5, 1985. Check your calendars, folks. August 5, 1985, was a Monday.

When Time Stood Still

Harry (Woody Harrelson) is called into the DA's office at 9:15 in *Palmetto* (1998). During a long conversation, the time on the clock never changes.

A Bad Swinger Bet

We've often said that the best flub spotters are those who know their stuff about a particular activity seen on film. Such was the case when a veteran gambler did a double-take during *Swingers* (1996). During the gambling scene, the boys are playing with black $100 chips. They buy in with $300, and get three chips. They bet one chip, and are dealt an eleven (a five and a six). Confronted with the problem of "doubling down," they can place one more chip and get another card in return. While they argue this among themselves, there's a shot of the cards, and two chips are already down. Then they place the second chip, and the dealer draws twenty-one.

Time Bombs

Sean Archer (John Travolta) is told that the bomb will go off in six days in *Face/Off* (1997). If that's the case, why does the bomb timer say 216-plus hours? That's nine days.

Increasing the Odds

If George Bush couldn't remember "the date that will live in infamy," should we fault Otto Preminger for recreating the Battle of Pearl Harbor for *In Harm's Way* (1965) with nine U.S. Navy battleships, one more than was actually there on December 7, 1941?

Where Are the Other Two?

King Kong (1933) has the great ape in chains on the New York stage (not a bad idea for some of the actors we've seen). Robert Armstrong comes out and recites a synopsis of the Skull Island adventure, saying that twelve of their party met horrible deaths. Actually, the count was ten. The dinosaur overturns a raft and kills three in the water plus the man who climbs the tree. Kong kills six more when he shakes them off a long branch into a ravine. The other deaths were residents of Skull Island.

The Ocean Breeze Did Him Good

Then again, King Kong is eighteen feet tall when he's on Skull Island, built to a one-foot-to-one-inch scale. But in New York, he's twenty-four feet tall. See what an ocean cruise can do for you?

How Many Women From Where?

Then again, *Seven Women From Hell* (1961) is not the kind of horror movie that title implies. It's actually about female prisoners of war. Six of them.

I'll Bet the Guys in Precinct 13 Were Glad

Did anyone notice that the *Assault on Precinct 13* (1976) was actually an attack on Precinct 9? Yep. And was Russian director Mikhail Romm aware that his film, *The Thirteen* (1936), was supposedly about a desert patrol of thirteen soldiers—except that there were only twelve?

The Sharpest Eye of the Year

Reader Bernard J. Sussman noticed that at the end of the credits of *Cold Comfort Farm* (1995), the copyright notice read "MCMXV," which would translate to 1915. Not bad, except that it's a story about the 1920's, from a book written in 1932. The correct copyright would be either MCMXCV or MVM, either of which would read 1995.

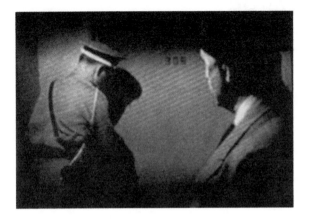 

Maybe the Six Was Upside Down

Klaatu the alien is shot and admitted to Room 306 of Walter Reed Hospital in *The Day the Earth Stood Still* (1951). Later, when he's talking to Professor Barnhardt, he says he stayed in Room 309.

THE SPELLING BE
(OR IS IT BEE? OR BEA?)

Now it's time to act like an old codger. If there's anything that riles us up, it's the fact that correct spelling seems to be a lost art. Hardly a day goes by that we don't spot a misspelling or incorrect usage in a newspaper, on a department store sign, or in an advertisement. Whatever happened to spelling?

Spell-checkers are part of the culprit. They can catch an error in the actual spelling, but unless they're very sophisticated, can't tell the difference between homophones (e.g., *to, too,* and *two; seen, scene; fore* and *four;* you get the message). It takes a thinking human to make sure that the spelling is contextually correct.

Of course, some spelling errors require a bit of knowledge of films and actors. Perhaps the star whose name is most often misspelled is Katharine Hepburn. It's often spelled Katherine, which is fine for some, but it just isn't the way she spells it. Look for a full-screen "Katherine Hepburn" in *State of the Union* (1948). Care should be taken.

End of sermon. Look for these games with names and with spelling from some of your favorite films:

Send in the "A" Team

On the ads for the original release of the star-studded *The Longest Day* in 1962, Robert Wagner, Fabian, Paul Anka and Tommy Sands are prominently pictured storming the beach at Normandy, but in the film's 1969 reissue, superimposed atop their uniformed likenesses (to appeal, apparently, to a more mature audience) are the heads of Richard Burton, Robert Mitchum, John Wayne and Henry Fonda.

A Pint of Guinness, Please

It was one of his greatest roles—Alec Guinness' dedicated, often single-minded Colonel in *Bridge on the River Kwai* (1957). However, the closing crawl for the seven-Oscar blockbuster spells Sir Alec's name as "Guiness," and the gaffe is compounded in many written articles about him. (Liza Minnelli frequently encounters a similar problem—as in the ads for the reissue of *New York, New York* where her last name had only one "n".)

And...while we're at it, you might like to know that since the actual writers who wrote the screenplay for *Bridge on the River Kwai* (Carl Foreman and Michael Wilson) were blacklisted during the nefarious McCarthy Era, the script is credited to novelist Pierre Boulle (who reportedly neither wrote nor spoke English). It was even to Boulle that the Academy of Motion Picture Arts and Sciences gave the Oscar for Best Screenplay—an oversight that was corrected two decades later. However, the credits say that the screenplay is "based on the novel of the same title." Boulle's novel, however, was titled "Bridge *Over* the River Kwai."

Fu Who?

One of the leading characters in the 1968 Christopher Lee movie, *The Castle of Fu Manchu*, is referred to as "Ingrid" in the film, "Anna" in the printed synopsis in press handouts, and "Maria" in the end credits.

A Back of the Hand to Cecil

In both the opening and closing credits of the memorable 1940 horror flick, *The Mummy's Hand*, Cecil Kellaway has to endure the indignity of having his name misspelled twice—as Kelloway. He probably should have slapped the mummy's hand!

Lynch the Person Who Wrote the Credits

The credits for the Ku Klux Klan drama *Black Legion* (1936), starring Humphrey Bogart, list Joe Sawyer and Helen Flint playing the roles of Cliff Moore and Pearl Davis. The names of the characters actually were Cliff Summers and Pearl Danvers.

King Luis

Just what kind of power does a director have when he can't even get his own named spelled correctly in the credits? The 1935 *Charlie Chan in Egypt* lists director Louis King as "Luis."

They're Not Who You Think They Are

Abbott and Costello call each other by their real names—"Bud" and "Lou"—throughout *Abbott and Costello Meet the Mummy* (1955). But the closing credits identify Bud as playing "Pete Patterson" and Louis as "Freddie Franklin."

They Couldn't Tell Each Other Apart

Not even the great *Gone With the Wind* (1939) is without its credits problems, taking us into an interesting realm. It's normal for most of us to have difficulty telling which twin is which. But is it also a problem for the twins themselves? George Reeves, who later became Superman, played one of the Tarleton twins and is identified in the opening credits as "Brent." However, when the twins talk with Scarlett O'Hara about the upcoming barbecue at Twelve Oaks, Reeves points to his twin brother (Fred Crane) and calls him "Brent."

Joker-ing Aside

The label on the bottle the Joker is hawking in the 1989 *Batman* is a dead giveaway that the movie was British-made: note the spelling of "moisturizing" with the English *s*.

Birdy, Do You Have the Times?

Even the master of deductive reasoning can slip up occasionally. In Billy Wilder's *The Private Life of Sherlock Holmes* (1970), Robert Stephens says that a newspaper in the bottom of a bird cage is "The Inverness Courier," but when the camera moves in for a closer look, it's "The Inverness Times."

An International Metropolis

Superman's Metropolis was actually in England during the filming of *Superman IV: Quest for Peace* (1987). Perhaps that's why the *Daily Planet* is identified as "Your Favourite Newspaper" (the British spelling of "favorite"). Also, while we are to assume that the subway chase scene takes place in New York, it's easy to see that it was shot in the London Underground, with its round tunnels, straphangers, and uniquely-shaped cars.

ACCIDENTAL ACTORS

Whenever we are interviewed for an article, radio, or TV show, the question "What's your favorite flub?" always arises. It's hard to pick a favorite, since we get a kick out of them all. But we do have a favorite *type* of flub. They fall into the category we call "Meet the Crew." We love to catch a crew member caught in a shot, and, more often than not, it's in a reflection.

Nothing does more to plunk you into reality while watching a movie than seeing a crew member. So, we present, from our favorite category:

Chasing the Reflection

When Holden (Ben Affleck) is walking back to his car in the rain in *Chasing Amy* (1997), look for the camera operator's reflection in a storefront window.

How to Make the Actors Scream

You have to wonder if the film crew was trying to sneak up on the actors in *Scream* (1996). You can see them reflected in the door of the police station, as well as in shadow in a bathroom.

Not as Deserted as You Think

A long shot in *Mysterious Island* (1961) establishes that when a hot-air balloon is downed, the cast is on a deserted island—deserted except for a crewman who darts behind a rock in the background.

A Shot in the Dark

When the punks drive up to a house enroute to terrorize the occupants early in Stanley Kubrick's chilling *A Clockwork Orange* (1971), watch as a crew person darts out of the shot in the dark background.

Down at the Station, Early in the Morning, See the Camera Crew

As Devereaux (Patrick McGoohan) burns the Rembrandt letters in his compartment in *Silver Streak* (1976), the train begins to pull out of the station. As you'd expect, the station seems to move away as the train moves. But instead of the train itself being reflected in the station's windows, you see a handcar containing a camera crew—filming the rear-screen projection that you're *really* seeing.

Wizardry They Didn't Count On

The shiny silver helmet that Nicol Williamson wears as the wizard Merlin in *Excalibur* (1981) performs a bit of wizardry on its own, showing us the cameraman in a scene near the end of the film.

Falling in Love With a Reflection

The camera can be seen in a mirror in the Meryl Streep–Robert De Niro romance *Falling in Love* (1984).

Not So Alone in the Woods

Albert Popwell stops his car in a wooded area where Clint Eastwood as Dirty Harry is shooting at a silhouette target in *Sudden Impact* (1983). The two are supposedly alone in the woods—except for the cameraman, whom you can see in a quick reflection in the car's vent window.

Titanic

We have a long tradition of "Picking on the Biggies," finding multiple flubs in the biggest movie blockbusters. The tradition moves to a new level as we pick on the biggest of biggies, that big movie that grossed big bucks and featured big stars and was about a big ship and had some big flubs.

There's been much debate about *Titanic*'s flubs, and many are questionable. Some of the messages we've had range from the ridiculous to the sublime. Ridiculous: why did Jack (Leonardo DiCaprio) mention having seen something (on, at) Nickelodeon when not only was there no TV, the kids' channel hadn't been invented yet. Simple. He was talking about a type of movie theater known as a "nickelodeon" which was popular at the time. Sublime: some folks complained that there was smoke coming out of the ship's fourth smokestack, which was pretty much for cosmetic purposes on the original ship. However, it was used as kitchen exhaust, so some coal smoke could have been coming from it. And in one of the flyover shots, you can see that much of the fourth stack is sealed.

But others bear more discussion. The dialogue has come in for its share of errors, not the least of which is Jack's referring to his having fished at Lake Wissota near Chippewa Falls, Wisconsin. The folks there were so delighted about the mention of their burg that they ordered up a key to the city for DiCaprio. Turns out that Lake Wissota was man-made, and not built until five years after the *Titanic*'s 1912 sinking. Jack leapt into the future with another line, when he mentioned a visit to the Santa Monica Pier. Maybe it was just a little jetty then, because the Santa Monica pier that we here in Los Angeles know and love was not built until 1916.

When the people at the dinner party are snooty, Jack looks to the future and brings forth a rather modern quote: "Someday, I hope people will be judged not by the color of their money but the content of their character." Then there's the nod to Peter, Paul, and Mary when Rose asks Jack if he will escape the ship. "The answer, Rose my friend," he says, "is blowing on the high seas."

There's been much ado about the authenticity of "Nearer, My God to Thee" being the final song sung as the ship descended, and we aren't going to go too deeply (ahem) into that one. But another problem was when they sang "Eternal Father, Strong to Save" with the verse: "Save all who dare the eagle's flight/And keep them by they watchful care/From every peril in the air." We're a little surprised about their concern for air safety, given that it wasn't much of a concern in 1912. We're even more surprised that they used that particular verse, which was written by Robert Nelson Spencer in 1937.

Another in the "sublime" category has to do with a particular wheel turn. When the ship is coming onto the iceberg, the officer of the watch shouts "hard a'starboard," whereupon the wheelman turns the wheel to port. Even though it sounds like an error, it probably wasn't. At the time of the *Titanic*, the ship's wheel acted much like a tiller. In a smaller boat with a tiller, you would turn the tiller right (starboard) to make the boat go left (port), and vice versa. Later on, ships would be steered much in the same manner as automobiles: turn left, go left, turn right, go right. Director James Cameron has said that he decided to go for accuracy, even though he knew there might be some confusion.

The "paintings" scene has created some interesting discussions, also. Both Picasso's *Les Demoiselles d'Avignon,* a Degas ballerina, and Claude Monet's *Water Lilies* were among Rose's collection. However, since you can see these very paintings in museums today, they apparently didn't go down with the ship. Some say that they could have been preliminary studies. Others say it's a goof. We assume the latter.

Here's one of those "amaze your friends" facts: the hands that actually draw Rose are a bit too old looking to belong to DiCaprio. That's because they're director Cameron's hands.

Another painting inconsistency which apparently couldn't be helped is that the Norman Wilkinson painting over the fireplace in the first-class smoking lounge is a view of the New York harbor actually painted for the Olympic, *Titanic's* sister ship. Wilkinson painted a Plymouth Harbor scene for the Titanic, but no representations of it survive.

There are a couple of physical errors that are relatively prominent. The draft markings on the bow are vastly different from one shot to another when Jack watches the dolphins swim by. A gross goof is that when he shows Rose how to spit, he turns one way with no spittle on his chin, but as he spins around a drip of drool is there. And how come the metal whistle Rose uses near the end doesn't freeze to her lips if it's wet and below freezing?

A mailbag is marked "Delivering to New York City—United States Postal Service—Via Royal Mail Service." Our post office was known as the United States Post Office Department (USPOD) until 1971, when it became the USPS.

We always enjoy an on-screen opportunity to meet the crew of a major motion picture. *Titanic* gives us the opportunity at least twice—once reflected on the TV set in Rose's home, and again when Jack makes his formal entrance into the dining room. When a butler opens the door for him, in the glass you can see a cameraman with his hand-held Steadicam camera.

Enough picking on *Titanic*. It's a big film, with more than a few flubs. But it's a masterpiece, and well worth the box office records it has set. And we hope James Cameron will be more gentle with us than he was with the *Los Angeles Times* film critic who trashed his movie. We liked it, Jim. We liked it. You're the king of the world!

OOPSIES: DEFYING CATEGORIZATION

Some things that happen either physically in the picture or contextually in the script just don't fit neatly into the categories within which we usually organize these books. So they get their own niche—Oopsies. Most bring about a uniform reaction: You see them, you go, "Oops!"

From the Oopsies File:

The Magic Waterfall

Not only did John Voight's performance in *Anaconda* (1997) defy everything we've ever heard about good acting, but one scene even defied gravity. Just after Voight is thrown overboard, a waterfall in the background flows upward.

Not Necessarily Out of Service

We've always suspected that actors get privileges denied to ordinary mortals. From *As Good as It Gets* (1997), we discover that they get to ride buses that the rest of us don't. The bus that Carol (Helen Hunt) rides on her way to thank Melvin sports a route sign that says "Out of Service."

A Horse of a Not-So-Different Color

When they're discussing Lipizzaner stallions in *Crimson Tide* (1995), Captain Ramsey (Gene Hackman) says the magnificent white horses are Portuguese. Lieutennant Commander Hunter (Denzel Washington) says that they're Spanish. The truth is that they're an Austrian breed, with origins in Arabia, Denmark, Italy, and Spain.

They Called Him What?

We have a multilingual correspondent to thank for this one. In Bernardo Bertolucci's *Il Conformista* (1970), Marcello (Jean-Louis Trintignant) mentions his old professor and says of him, in Italian, "We called him Smerdyakov." The translators were thrown by the name, not knowing if it was French, Russian, or German. So the subtitle read "We called him shithead." Also, look for a radio tower when the movie flashes back to Marcello's boyhood in Rome in 1917.

Getting a Little Behind in His Work

As the revelers dance around during the "Baal" scene in *The Ten Commandments* (1956), watch closely and you'll see a goldsmith accidentally back into his hot smelter, burn himself, and jump quickly away.

Some Thieves Steal Jewels, Others Become Congressmen

It's always been difficult to tell the difference between thieves and politicians. Further evidence may be found in a headline in the *Washington Times*, seen in *Absolute Power* (1997). It reads "Jewel Thief Caught." But the text of the article is about congressional hearings.

And He Got a Kick Out of It, Too

Fans of *Star Wars* (1977) always get a kick out of an incident in the trash compactor scene. Luke Skywalker is trying to contact the 'droids from the control room when the storm troopers come in following Darth Vader. One of the charging troopers slams his head on the door frame and is knocked backwards. Sorta destroys your confidence in the invincibility of the white-armored warriors, doesn't it?

Lost In the Park

No wonder poor Dennis Nedry (Wayne Knight) gets attacked by the dinosaurs in *Jurassic Park* (1993). Maybe it's because it wasn't given any help from the directional signs as he's atop the miniature waterfall. In one shot, you see a sign reading "East Dock" with an arrow pointing to the right. But when he stumbles down, you see the sign again with the arrow pointing to the left. Then again, he always had problems with geography. When he's seen seated at a beachfront cafe there's a caption which says "San Jose, Costa Rica." San Jose is landlocked, without any adjoining bodies of water.

A Flub Called Wanda

We don't know if it's by accident or by design, but in the last scene of *Fierce Creatures* (1997), Rollo (John Cleese) calls Willa (Jamie Lee Curtis) "Wanda." Is it a slip-up from too much familiarity, or is it an inside joke referring to their earlier pairing as Archie and Wanda in *A Fish Called Wanda* (1988)? Your call.

The Boy Is a Bit Backward

The first time we see the Beaver's (Cameron Finley) football helmet in *Leave It to Beaver* (1997) the word AIR is backward, apparently the result of flipped film. In later shots it's back to normal.

A Highly Complex Flying Machine

A friend who is a veteran airline pilot says that he always keeps an eye out for "airplane flubs" in movies, and in a recent conversation even caught your Flubmeister in an aviation slipup in an earlier book (we're keeping it a secret). We just heard about a new one. It's in *Day of the Triffids* (1962).

There's a scene when Masen (Howard Keel) and Coker (Mervyn Johns) investigate the wreck of a small, tandem-seated, open cockpit airplane which crashed in a field due to engine failure. Maybe the real reason it crashed is that it fell off its chain. The airplane is from an amusement-park ride.

TV or Not TV, That Is the Question

We have to think about this one a bit. In *The Girl Can't Help It* (1956), Jayne Mansfield and Tom Ewell return to her townhouse and receive a frantic phone call from Jayne's mobster boyfriend (Edmond O'Brien), telling her to turn on the TV set to a certain channel. She does, and we see a color picture. In the 1950s color TV's were a rarity. We have to assume that a piece of color film was rear-projected onto a fake TV on the set. Let this serve as a warning to the colorizers when they see a TV picture in an old black-and-white movie! Touch not that screen.

Batman Can't Spell

Batman (1989) had more than its share of prop spelling problems, as detailed in *FILM FLUBS*. Yet another has been unearthed: On the menus next to the tables in the museum restaurant, the spelling is "Fluegelheim Museum." On a sign, an "e" is lost and it becomes "Flugelheim Museum."

Ask Not for Whom the Anvil Tolls

Yet another flub spotter who watched the filming of *Glory* (1989) in Savannah reveals director Edward Zwick's ingenious solution when confronted with background noise. It seems that a new bridge was being built over the Savannah River not far away, and a pile driver was making a prodigious noise. Directors have, of course, all kinds of power, but stopping construction on a bridge project might just be outside the realm of possibility. So Zwick put a blacksmith in the background, hitting an anvil in perfect time with each strike of the pile driver.

A Rank Problem

In the opening scenes of *Glory* (1989), Matthew Broderick says how proud he is to have been made captain. He has two bars on his shoulders, indicating that rank. But in the next shot they're gone, dropping him back to second lieutenant. Still later the bars are back again.

And we just can't leave *Glory* alone. Well, when a movie is this fine, it's even more fun to find its cinema slipups. A favorite in this corner: As his regiment marches through a Southern town, Morgan Freeman stops to talk to some children. When he leaves to rejoin his regiment, they wave to him, but as they raise their hands, notice that the youngest on the far right is wearing a digital watch.

One more and we're through: When the regiment goes into battle for the first time, notice that in one shot their rifles have no bayonets, in another they do, then they're gone again, but back again later during hand-to-hand combat.

The Spare Box

Alan Ladd, while seated on a high porch in *Whispering Smith* (1949), takes a harmonica out of his inside coat pocket, throws away the box, then plays a tune. When he's finished, he reaches back into his pocket, takes out another box, and puts the harmonica into it.

SOUNDS LIKE A PROBLEM TO ME

Getting sounds and sound effects right is a complex part of the movie business. Often the sound recorded on the set just doesn't work because of background noise and other problems. Or there can be the problem of getting a microphone close enough to an actor to record the sound. If the mike needs to be so close that it shows up in the shot, it's better to record a reference track from afar, then go back to a recording studio and re-record the dialogue while looking at the picture (a technique called *looping*).

Then there are the sounds which just don't sound right. Our ears are trained to associate certain sounds with certain actions and, oddly enough, when the real sound is recorded for a particular scene or action, it might not be what we expect. So the filmmakers go to a Foley Stage and make things sound the way we think they should.

There's another problem, too. If you're shooting a gunfight scene in a certain neighborhood at night, you don't want to wake up the town. So you shoot it with guns that make flaring lights but little sound, then put in the bangs later. Alternatively, an on-set explosion might not be nearly as noisy as you want it to be. So you film the explosion, then add a tapestry of sound to it later.

Of course, you can't actually *shoot* the actors (even though there are many directors who would like very much to do so). So Foley artists shoot a bullet into a side of beef to record a gunshot sound, or smash a watermelon to approximate a head being hit. That's just the way it has to be.

Given all that explanation, things still don't sound just right, as in these instances:

It's Not Jake With Us

Big Jake's (John Wayne) son Michael (Chris Mitchum) rides a very old motorcycle in the Western, *Big Jake* (1971). In fact, a biking enthusiast pointed out that this motorcycle is one of the first ever produced, perhaps a very old Harley Davidson. But the sound is that of a modern Japanese bike. And in a close-up, you can see that the old American bike is powered by a very modern Japanese engine.

It's Not Jake II (The Two Jakes)

Likewise, near the end of *Black Rain* (1989), another motorcycle enthusiast, with an ear for that sort of thing, reported that Michael Douglas and a bad guy are chasing through a field on two-stroke, one-cylinder dirt bikes. But the sound is that of a four-stroke motor.

One Hell of an Echo

Nick and Nora Charles are at a nightclub celebrating New Year's Eve in *After the Thin Man* (1936), where a chanteuse is singing "Smoke Dreams." After finishing, she is seen leaving the club with a man. A few scenes later, Nick and Nora are in the owner's office using the telephone, and just as the sequence ends, you can hear the chanteuse still singing "Smoke Dreams," even though she previously had left the club.

Oklahoma Crude... Really Crude

Excuse us for a moment of crudity. In *Oklahoma Crude* (1973), director Stanley Kramer must have opted to yield to the MPAA ratings mavens rather than stick to the script as recorded. Faye Dunaway is talking to George C. Scott over a meal. Scott taunts her for being tough and masculine. He asks her if she'd prefer having a man's genitals or a woman's. She replies, "Both." Then he sets himself up by asking "Why?" Now watch her lips as she says, "Because if I had both, I could fuck myself." But that's not what you'll hear. To appease the MPAA, Kramer had Dunaway loop the line to say "screw myself." But the lips don't lie.

Yo, Olivia! We Can't Hear You!

When Michael Beck and Gene Kelly are conversing up close during the reconstruction of the auditorium in *Xanadu* (1980), the camera shows

Olivia Newton-John talking to them off in the distance, but you don't hear a word. The two turn and say something to her. Did someone on the crew forget to turn on her mike?

An Improper Introduction

Tom Cruise plays race driver Cole Trickle in *Days of Thunder* (1990). When he meets Cary Elwes, as his rival Russ Wheeler, and Russ's wife as they walk alongside a lake, she greets him with "Hi, Tom."

NOT QUITE DEAD ENOUGH

Playing dead is a talent that has been refined by dogs and opossums, but still is a little difficult for actors. It's tough to be a corpse. You can't breathe, you can't blink, you can't flinch. Or can you?

News From the Neighborhood

A Los Angeles reader noticed that in *Volcano* (1997) a fire truck from Station 23 in her own neighborhood is on its side, apparently destroyed. But a few scenes later it's unscathed and back on its way to help the unfortunate. And, as if you cared, in the final scene you can see the lava flow past your Flubmeister's own neighborhood, a few blocks from the Beverly Center Mall.

Not as Dead as You Think

Johnny (Vincent Gallo) is a corpse in Abel Ferrara's *The Funeral* (1996). His portrayal is made less convincing by the fact that he flinches when another character touches his eyebrow.

Back From the Dead (Again)

We've talked about the "undead" flubs in *The Abyss, The Boys From Brazil,* and a few others. Now there's one in Disney's hardware blockbuster, *Armageddon* (1998). When some of the crew members are killed in a shuttle crash on the asteroid, check out the late Oscar. When A. J. (Ben Affleck) finds him dead, the driller's eyes blink.

A Role to Die For

Paul Boller and Ronald L. Davis report in their delightful *Hollywood Anecdotes* an incident during the filming in 1934 of *The Thin Man.* A bevy of Metro character actors are seated around a refectory table for a long tracking shot by director W.S. "Woody" Van Dyke. A bespectacled veteran actor with a black mustache, at the head of the table, is delivering a long speech, as the camera trucks along, getting the reactions of each character. As the camera got to the end, the actor concluded, "And that's all I have to say," at which point he sat down and actually died. But Van Dyke reportedly wouldn't allow the body to be taken from the set until he had knelt behind the dead actor with his viewfinder and set up an over-the-shoulder shot. "All right, take him out, but leave the coat," he barked. Which garment he then put on another actor to finish the scene with over-the-shoulder shots.

The Dead Can Be Startled, Too

When divers enter the sunken submarine in *The Abyss* (1989), they are startled when they open a hatchway and a crewman's body comes floating toward them. The late crewman must have been a bit startled, too. Look closely and you'll see him blink when the bright light hits his face.

Feeling Good About Being Dead

Maybe we'd better think twice about Dan Aykroyd's mortuary in *My Girl* (1991). Are these people really dead, or is this a replay of *Murders in the Rue Morgue*? The body of the old schoolmarm appears to be breathing, as does that of young Thomas J. (Macauley Culkin).

Our flub-spotters are unforgiving. Someone noticed that when Thomas J.'s mother turns over Vada's (Anna Chlumsky) mood ring, which Thomas J. was holding, it's a bright turquoise, usually indicating that you feel pretty good. Remember mood rings? When they weren't worn in a while, away from body heat, they turned a motley blue/black.

Was It Involuntary Muscular Reactions?

When Robin Williams and the Lost Boys are fighting the pirates in *Hook* (1991), they kill a few, who move around after they're dead.

Alan Rickman Scares Me, Too

Bruce Willis sends a dead terrorist down the elevator shaft in *Die Hard* (1988). Dastardly Alan Rickman turns him over, and just as Rickman's hand nears his face, the startled corpse blinks.

BUTTONS AND BOWS,
BITS AND PIECES,
AND CHANGING CLOTHES

Movies are shot in bits and pieces, and maintaining costume continuity from shot to shot can be quite a challenge. The average "take" covers only a few seconds of the action, and an entire day's work may move the story along only a couple of minutes. The scene which is started today may be finished tomorrow, the next day, or even months later. To take advantage of set and location economies, scenes are often shot out of context—the end may well be filmed long before the beginning—and therein lies the opportunity for many a goof to slip into the footage.

We're not just talking low-budget specials, either. Costume glitches have crept into the classics, and they continue to pop up in many of today's big-budget blockbusters.

Changing of the Colors

In *North By Northwest* (1959), the only suit that Cary Grant carries with him is light blue-gray, when he's in the Chicago hotel; dark gray out on the prairie. Hitchcock said it wasn't an error—he blamed it on the lighting.

146

Swirling Skirts

In *Silk Stockings*, the 1957 musical remake of the classic *Ninotchka*, comely Russian Commissar Cyd Charisse wears a flowing gray skirt with a front seam sewn all the way to the hem. As she swirls and twirls with Fred Astaire, her attire changes from skirt to culottes and back again. In several of the dance turns, it's very obvious that she's wearing a skirt. In the scenes where she does splits and larger steps, the outfit is split into more modest culottes.

Easier on the Feet

Near the end of *The First Wives Club* (1996), Elise (Goldie Hawn) is wearing high heels with multiple straps during a dance number after a party at their offices. But when she walks out onto the street with Brenda (Bette Midler) and Annie (Diane Keaton), as she goes through the door her shoes change into more comfortable single-strap low heels for a stroll down the rough, cobblestone street.

A Fast Change of Shoes

When Madeline (Kim Novak) rushes up the stairs of Mission San Juan Bautista in Alfred Hitchcock's *Vertigo* (1958), she's wearing a gray suit with black heels. Yet when Elster (Tom Helmore) throws his wife from the tower and there's a close-up of the body, she's wearing white heels. Later, we see Elster holding the dead body, and she's back in the black heels. In the same scene, look for a crewperson's hand and forearm appearing for a few seconds as she heads up the stairs.

The Ties That (Don't) Bind

Something about having men from Mars drop in on the planet Earth seems to have unnerved President Dale (Jack Nicholson) in Tim Burton's *Mars Attacks* (1996). Near the end of the film, the President is trying to make peace with the Martians, using the now-hackneyed line, "Why can't we all just get along?" As he goes toward them, he tightens his tie. The Martian reacts, then in the next shot the tie is loose again. Then for the next few shots the tie alternates between being loose and tied. And watch Dr. Kessler's (Pierce Brosnan) pipe as he meets with the President. It alternates between being lit and unlit.

Imelda Would Be Proud of Her

Ann, the "Flower Lady" (Allison Janney), shows up for the climactic party in *Big Night* (1996) wearing a glamorous party dress, but her footwear is the same white sneakers she wore in an earlier scene. But moments later she dances in a pair of black high heels that she didn't bring with her, nor did she have time to change.

It's That Old Shirt Problem Again

One of filmdom's favorite flubs occurs in *Pretty Woman* (1990) when Julia Roberts tries to remove Richard Gere's tie during a love scene in their hotel room. She takes off his tie and unbuttons his collar, then in the next shot the tie's right back in place. Gere returns to the collar problem in *Primal Fear* (1996). Gere, playing Martin Vail, comes into a room wearing a buttoned-down collar, then a few shots later it's straight-pointed; then it's buttoned down again.

The Hat Trick, Parte Deux

As Lucy (Sadie Frost) helps Jack Seward (Richard E. Grant) onto the sofa after he trips on a bear rug in *Bram Stoker's Dracula* (1992), Quincy (Bill Campbell) is holding his own hat. In the next scene, Jack hands Quincy his hat and apologizes for sitting on it. Another fun flub happens after Seward is bitten by Renfield (Tom Waits), then holds the wrong side of his throat.

Damn the Continuity, Full Speed Ahead

Director Leo McCarey always cut for the funniest takes in a Marx Brothers movie, continuity be damned. Thus in *Duck Soup* (1933), in the opening reception for Rufus J. Firefly, Groucho's coat changes from gray with braids to tails and back again.

The Countess—Now Two Inches Shorter

Sophia Loren and Marlon Brando are in his stateroom on the ship in *A Countess From Hong Kong* (1967). Director Charlie Chaplin didn't notice that she started the scene wearing high heels and walked away at the end in flats.

Fallen on the Battlefield

Somebody caught it and fixed it, but not soon enough for one of Michael Lerner's military medals to create a very obvious flub in *Barton Fink* (1991). As Lerner, playing movie mogul Jack Lipnick, argues with John Turturro, in the title role, one of his campaign ribbons slips and dangles lopsidedly on its pin. In the next shot, it's neatly back in place.

Anatomy of an Error

There's a curious problem in Otto Preminger's 1959 *Anatomy of a Murder*. Oddly enough, Lana Turner had walked off the picture, and Preminger said that it was because she didn't like her costumes. Turner replied, "I would not walk out of a picture for anything as trivial as a costume." But Preminger, vowing to take a lesser "star" and make her "a new Lana Turner," cast Lee Remick in the role. The controversy must have broken the concentration of the costumers. Watch Remick as she prepares to leave the cafe in a pivotal scene. She sashays to the door wearing a lovely, flowing skirt, but coming out the door to the street, she has on tight-fitting slacks!

Numbers Game

In *Jailhouse Rock* (1957), Elvis Presley is seen at one point wearing uniform #6239; in another scene, his number magically becomes #6240. Was he promoted for good behavior or great rock 'n' rollin'?

The studio retouched this '41 publicity still for *Reap the Wild Wind*

...Just check the dude with the shades in the original.

TV TROUBLES

Searching out the goofs and screw-ups in television programs presents a real challenge. This is one arena wherein you have to be sharp of eye and quick of mind. It's fleeting flubdom. The gaffe you see flits away like a water sprite on electronic wings, and more often than not, unless you've taped the show, you don't have the opportunity to go back and take another look.

But our flub spotters are a bright and diligent lot. Some have an amazing talent, and we are pleased to report their findings:

An Early Research Project

Obviously, there was some research going on back in the 1800s, according to evidence in *Son of the Morning Star*, a 1991 TV-movie about General George Custer. When he's hunting a herd of bison, one wears a red eartag.

Arrest the Sheriff

In an early episode of *The Andy Griffith Show*, Sheriff Taylor takes his girlfriend, Peggy McMillan (Joanna Moore), to a Raleigh restaurant for dinner. He orders a beer, and she has a mixed drink. The scene makes the pair into lawbreakers, since North Carolina didn't allow the sale of liquor by the drink at the time the episode was set, the early 1960s.

The Ears Have It

Eagle-eyed flub spotters just won't let a director get away with anything. Take, for instance, what happened in a TV movie, *Girl of the Limberlost* (1991). Several farmers noticed the heroine is picking seed corn during a storm. The ears she is picking and the stalks they come from are a lush green. However, she's actually picking roasting ears (corn on the cob). Seed corn is picked in the fall after the stalks and ears are dry and brown.

Alice Doesn't Ring There Anymore

Alice gets a telephone in the January 26, 1956, episode, "The Baby Sitter," of *The Honeymooners*. The number is BEnsonhurst 3-7741. However, between the original airing and the time the show went into syndication, it must have been discovered that it was someone's real number. In the syndicated version, even though you can see Jackie Gleason mouthing the original number, the number you hear is BEnsonhurst 3-5555.

Vinnie and Sonny...No Thelma and Louise

In the climactic episode of the famed six "arc" *Wiseguy* TV action-adventure, the setting is a movie house on New Jersey's south shore. The place is being locked up for the winter, as we see in the opening scene. Shortly thereafter, suave gangster Sonny Steelgrave (Ray Sharkey) manages to find his way in, figuring it's a good hideout from the feds who are pursuing him. Our hero, Vinnie Terranova (Ken Wahl), tracks him there and confronts him—over a bag of hot popcorn and a candy bar, before the two engage in fisticuffs, resulting in Sonny's electrocution when he is backed into some exposed wires. Our question is: if the place was closed for the season and locked up, why was the electricity left on, the popcorn machine poppin' away, and the concessions counter still packed with neatly displayed goodies?

Finding Time When You Need It

Calum (John McGlynn) tells James Herriot (Christopher Timothy) that he must rush to the train station in *All Creatures Great and Small* (1975), saying that he's going to pick up his girlfriend and doesn't have time to stand and talk with him. But he must have found time to change his shirt and tie, because they're different from what he was wearing a few moments before.

The Multi-Level Mohawk

Watch for varying heights of Mr. T's mohawk in episodes of *The A-Team*. Apparently his hairstylist didn't have a ruler.

Mladen…What a Fun Guy

Veteran actor Karl Malden, né Mladen Sekulovich, for years worked his own in-joke into whatever he was doing. On his *Streets of San Francisco* TV series, he invariably would take a moment during a dressing down of someone or other in his office to open the door and bark, "Get me a cup of coffee, Sekulovich!" to some unseen actor. And in one of his TV movies, *Word of Honor* (1981), while conversing with someone on the sidewalk, an extra walking by bumps him accidentally. Whereupon Malden, annoyed, yells after him, "Watch it, Sekulovich!"

Who Took the Jacket?

A jacket is hanging on a peg on the mirror when Tony Danza walks by in *Who's the Boss?* In the next shot, the jacket has mysteriously disappeared.

Weird Boston Weather

An episode of *Spenser: For Hire* has Robert Urich and his associate engaged in conversation, during which it is snowing in the close-ups, but not in the long shots.

The Confederate Faith Healer

Orry Main (Patrick Swayze) has a scar under one eye as he talks to President Jefferson Davis in *North and South, Part II*—but the scar heals and vanishes during the scene. Wonder if he had to make a "love offering" in Confederate dollars?

The Confederacy, Part II

In one of the old *Rin Tin Tin* episodes, two Civil War generals are having a sword fight on the steps of the courthouse. Suddenly two men in business suits walk out the door, look startled—as if someone told them to get off the set—and run out of the picture.

We're Talking Dead Drunk

An early 1990 episode of *L.A. Law* had Harry Hamlin representing a drunk driver. At one point, Hamlin said that the driver's breath test indicated an alcohol level of ".90." Later in the episode, it was corrected to ".09." Someone with a .90 level would either be dead or comatose. Our spotter wrote to *L.A. Law*, and the show 'fessed up to the error.

The Oddball Getaway

In the 1991 thriller, *Fever*, Armand Assante and Sam Neill are chasing all over town to get phone messages from the kidnapper of their mutual girlfriend. Ultimately they drive up to one phone booth in a single car, get the latest instructions, and then drive off in two separate cars. There was a car conveniently sitting there with the motor running! Later in the same film, Assante is temporarily stunned when taking a bullet just above the heart(!), then spends the remaining footage with blood dripping down his *right* arm.

An Early, Early Hank Williams Tune

The Virginian was set in the 1890s; but in an episode which introduces Randy Boone to the cast, he sings "I'm So Lonesome I Could Cry." Not bad. Hank Williams, who wrote the song, wasn't born until 1923.

Those Damned Specs

In the TV-movie, *Face of a Stranger* (1991), Gena Rowlands and Harris Yulin meet for lunch in a restaurant. In the first shot, over his shoulder looking at her, Yulin is seen adjusting his glasses to read the menu. In the opposite shot following, over her shoulder looking at him, he's just taking the glasses out of his inside coat pocket. The third shot, once again over his shoulder, finds him still fiddling with and adjusting his glasses that he is wearing.

Two Changes Make a Full House

In *Full House*, John Stamos's character name changed from Jesse Cochran to Jesse Katsapolous after the first season. Howcum? Did he change ethnicity also? In another show, little Stephanie (Jodie Sweetin) lost a baby tooth—but by the next show, it was back, full sized. Even though our reader wonders about this, we suspect that it was because most sitcom child parts are played by identical twins, to maintain a shooting schedule in compliance with child labor laws—and one had lost the tooth, the other hadn't.

Shannon's Mis-Deal

Elizabeth Peña plays a secretary, Lucy, in television's *Shannon's Deal*, but in a 1991 episode, twice Shannon (Jamey Sheridan) called her "Elizabeth"—once saying, "Will you come here, Elizabeth?"

What the 'L?

Supered over an establishing shot of a Nebraska town in *Lonesome Dove* (1989) is the name "Ogalalla." A later scene opens with a pan of a sign in the town, which now read, "Ogallala." The latter is the correct spelling.

The Diablo Made Me Do It

HBO's made-for-tv movie *El Diablo* (1990) is supposedly set in the Old West, yet in an aerial view, cars can be seen in the bottom of a valley.

A Yuletide Story

Our friend Bob Zeschin owns up to a flub in a Christmas movie he wrote—the wonderful *Story Lady* (1991), with Jessica Tandy. One of his characters is mentioned as having a MBA degree from Yale. Later, he found that Yale has no MBA program.

The Continuity Bombed Out, Also

An elderly couple plant a bomb in their car to blow it up as a protest in a *Starsky and Hutch* episode, but thieves steal the car, and our heroes must retrieve it before the bomb explodes.

A car buff noticed that when the car is stolen, it's a 1963 Chevy Impala two-door hardtop. When the thieves remove the masking paper after repainting it, it's a 1964 Impala two-door sedan. When the police dispatcher reports it stolen, he calls it a 1973 Chevy. Then, when the car finally explodes, it's a 1963 Chevy Bel Air two-door sedan.

The Set Designer Was No Hero

It's set in World War II, of course, and in an episode of *Hogan's Heroes*, Colonel Hogan (Bob Crane) is secretly flown to England during the night, just before D-Day. In the background, there's map showing both East and West Germany— a split that didn't happen until after the war.

The Wet Address—and Other "Lucy" Flubs

At the risk of besmirching an icon, our first look is at the wonderful *I Love Lucy* series. We're on fairly solid ground here, since the *Lucy* flubs were supplied by Bart Andrews, perhaps the world's leading authority on

the work of Lucille Ball, author of three books on her, and consultant to Universal Studios on their *I Love Lucy* tribute attraction.

"There's a blooper or two in just about every one of the 179 episodes," Andrews says, and he shares his favorites.

He reports that if you go to New York to look for the Ricardo's home, you might need scuba gear. In the series, Lucy and Desi lived at 623 East 68th Street. That particular location happens to be in the middle of the East River.

Even more fun is finding all of Ethel's middle names. "Ethel Mertz had three different middle names," Bart reports, "the result of overworked scriptwriters who didn't have time to go back and check previous scripts. For trivia buffs, the middle monikers were Louise, Mae, and Vivian Vance's real middle name, Roberta."

How about the time that the Ricardos moved a few doors down the hall without really changing apartments? The writers surreptitiously changed Lucy and Ricky's apartment number from 3-B to 3-D so they could make a joke about three-dimensional movies. But when the episode was over, the new number remained on the apartment door.

Lucy teaches Ethel to drive in an episode which comes a couple of years *after* one in which Ethel talks about following Lucy in a station wagon.

"More than once," Bart adds, "a musician in Desi Arnaz's orchestra would refer to the leader as 'Desi,' not 'Ricky.' Rather than do expensive retakes, they'd decided to just let it slide, justifying their decision by probably reasoning that TV would probably be a fleeting fad."

The Fugitive—Running Away From His Flubs

Finally, we dissect *The Fugitive* TV series—one which has also taken on cult status. We have fan Linda Rogers to thank for a list of things that bothered her in the series:

The numerous writers couldn't agree on whether fugitive Richard Kimble's wife (whom he had been convicted of killing) had been strangled or bludgeoned, even though the flashbacks at the beginning of each program show that she was hit with a lamp. In the final episode the one-armed man confirms that he hit her.

The time frame seems to indicate that Kimble was indeed an over-achiever. Let's see if we can add it up: When his wife is killed, he is thirty-three. By that time, according to various episodes, he has completed college, medical school, an internship, two residencies, and two years in Korea as a medic, and built up a successful practice. Let's see—if he got out of college at twenty-two (assuming he started at eighteen), then had four years of medical school, that's twenty-six. Then a year of intern-ship—twenty-seven; two residencies at two years each (guess)—thirty-one; two years in Korea—thirty-three. So when did he get around to starting the practice?

The Fugitive stops at the Edmund Hotel in Kansas City, Sioux Falls, and various other cities. Was it a national chain, or an inside joke?

In a first-season two-parter, the title word twice is misspelled "Lonley."

In the final episode, Kimble and the one-armed man duke it out atop a ride in an abandoned amusement park—beside which is a healthy palm tree. Even though the ride is called "Mahi Mahi," can a palm tree survive in Indiana?

The Fugitive, with a wounded Norma Crane in tow, runs all over the place to escape the police in episode 56, finally ending up in a construction hut. Along the way he changes socks several times, from light to dark. Now, that's being fastidious. But after all, he's a doctor trained in hygiene. Of course, he doesn't wash his hands until *after* he performs kitchen surgery in episode 103.

In episode 106 there's a tense moment when guest star John Larch calls his son (Beau Bridges) by the name that the Fugitive is using.

And we conclude on a more intimate note: In the first place, throughout the series, David Janssen is forever tripping on things, stumbling, backing into things, and having near-misses which, perhaps, can be attributed to his oft-reported heavy drinking and his bum leg. Of course, most of the dangerous work was done by a stunt man who bore very little resemblance to Janssen other than being male.

Our faithful correspondent also noticed that in episode 93, something might well have been going on in the dressing room trailer between takes. She thought that he was walking down the street with a golf ball in the left front pocket of his polyester pants. But she called in her husband, himself a golfer of the polyester pants generation, who took a look at the tape and pointed out that it was no golf ball—it was certainly an aroused actor. Sorta recalls the old Mae West line from *She Done Him Wrong* (1933)—"Is that a gun in your pocket, or are you just glad to see me?"

Mugato...Gumato...Either Way, It's a Mean Sucker

In the *Star Trek* episode "A Private Little War," a creature on the planet Neural is called a "Mugato" by Captain Kirk, one ever-diligent flub spotter noticed. Later, Nona (Nancy Kovack) calls the same creature a "Gumato." Either way, it's a mean sucker, our spotter reports.

Miss-M*A*S*H'es

In one episode of the popular TV series, *M*A*S*H*, a wounded G.I. shoots a Chinese soldier who is trying to steal boots. Later they become friends at the 4077th, where the American gives the enemy soldier a Hershey Bar as a gesture of friendship. The candy bar has a bar code on the wrapper—a computerization phenomenon that wasn't around until decades after the Korean War.

And in another episode, Colonel Blake is on the phone talking about the movies that they are showing. He says, "We only got *The Thing* and *The Blob*." The Korean War lasted from 1950 to 1953; they may well have had *The Thing*, since it was released in 1951. But *The Blob* didn't ooze out until 1958.

The Search for the Right Skyline

Manhunt: The Search for the Night Stalker (1989) is a made-for-TV movie which takes place in Los Angeles during a 1985 serial murder case. In the background, you can see the newly built Library Tower (okay, it's really the First Interstate World Center, but no red-blooded Angeleno calls it by that corporate gobbledygook). It's the tallest building in the West, but was nowhere near completion in 1985.

Where Wise Men Fear to Trek

Deal with a series as popular as both the TV and film emanations of *Star Trek* , with its legions of fans who know each episode frame by frame, and you're sure to do some Trekkie toe treading. Actually, many of the devotees of the series came forward to share their favorite *Star Trek* flubs. Glitches and goof-ups from the *Trek* films are dealt with elsewhere in this book. But now it's time to take a look at the TV series. Fools rush in...

In an episode entitled "The Alternative Factor," notice how actor Robert Brown's goatee ranges from grown to partially grown to sparse with just a few strands of hair.

Leonard Nimoy is seen meditating in a close-up in the "Amok Time" episode. A cut to a wide shot shows him casually leaning against the wall in the background, then the next cut shows him meditating again.

The crew is attacked by a World War II fighter in "Shoreleave." When the plane is first seen, it's a U. S. Navy Corsair (recognizable by its gull-wing configuration and U. S. military markings). In the close-ups, the plane is a Japanese Zero.

As Guinan (Whoopi Goldberg) and Geordie (LeVar Burton) play chess in the *Star Trek: The Next Generation* episode "Galaxy's Child," the camera angles change, and so do the numbers and positions of the pieces on the 3-D chess board.

Trekkin' Right Along...

In an interesting bit of cross-pollination from the TV series to the filmed version, in *Star Trek II: The Wrath of Khan* (1982), Ricardo Montalban (Khan) says he "never forgets a face" as he recognizes Walter Koenig (Chekov). Montalban is referring to the TV episode "Space Seed" in which he guested as Khan. However, Koenig was not a member of the cast when the "Space Seed" episode was filmed.

Were They Having a Shaving Cream Fight?

In an episode of *Moonlighting*—one which, oddly enough, won the Emmy for editing—Davis Addison (Bruce Willis) runs into Maddie's (Cybill Shepherd) office in an undershirt and red and white boxers with shaving cream on his face. In the subsequent banter the shaving cream is alternately spread over his face or mostly wiped off.

The Sharp-Eyed Flub Spotter Squad

Once again, we have to thank the thousands of readers who have written us to share the flubs they've spotted while watching movies either in the theaters or at home, as well as those who call in when we're guesting on radio and television shows. Unfortunately, most of the callers we know only by their first names, so we can only express our gratitude for your anonymous contributions as well as the pleasure we get from speaking with you. The Internet has opened up a new world of flub-spotting, and in addition to the "snail mail" we continue to receive, rarely a day goes by that we don't hear from someone via e-mail, often from some distant part of the globe. If the e-mails were signed with a full name, it's included here. We're deliberately not listing those which were signed only with an e-mail address "handle," choosing not to expose your address to the lame-brained "spammers" who fill your e-mail box with trash. We've tried to list all of you who contributed to this book, as well as a few who contributed items which weren't acknowledged in *Roman Soldiers Don't Wear Watches*. Due to editing exigencies, the item you contributed may have vanished as the book was being assembled. Also, since you're so sharp-eyed and generous with your sharing (and please don't stop!) we receive many duplicates of the same flub. Wherever possible, we try to acknowledge the earliest contributor, but the system ain't perfect. We try. If you see a flub in the book that you sent in and your name isn't here, perhaps you weren't the first, but we really appreciate your efforts, and the odds are very high that you'll be in a future volume. Since some of the flubs herein are reprinted from *Film Flubs, Son of Film Flubs,* and *Film Flubs: The Sequel,* hopefully they're acknowledged in those volumes; there was no way we could sort out all the names and repeat them here.

Most of all, thanks so much for your many cards, letters, and e-mails telling us how much you enjoy the books. They make it all worthwhile.

—Bill Givens

Robyn Aaronson, Keith Adams, Shannon Adams, Lynn Alman, Jay Anderson, Bart Andrews, Julie Barman, Corey Becker, Leah Bender, Kevin A. Boehm, Jr., Joe Bott, Fred Brice, Cindy Britton, Nancy Bryan, Donna Cannon, Doug Carlson, Karien-io Chow, James Clink, Michael A. Coan, Edward Cogan, Charlene Cohan, Edward Cohen, Jim Coston, Lowell Deo, Paul Dial, Will Dial, Steve Dunshee, Chris Eichers, Donald A. Eisner, Autumn Fontenot, Raymond Garrison, Rob Goald, William Gravitz, Mauu Grieg, Josh Gross, Hodel, H. I. George M. Harrington, Jr., Brooke Harris, Roy Harris, Jodi Higginson, Steven Holmes, Ryan Howell, John Huber, Bob Jenson, Dave Johnson, David M. Johnston, Helen Keene, Joey Keene, Ben Kempner, Anna Kilgore, Jason Knox, Joe Kölb, Bev Kutnick, David Lachance, Andrew Lacker, Brian Laik, David Lean, Jeff Lentz, Saren Leono, William A. Marcolongo, Susan J. Marier, Ben McDaniel, John McKenzie, Bob Melton, Rick Miller, Les Mims, Patricia Munro, Dunlap, N. M. J. P. Nacy, Julie Nichols, John Novellino, Don O'Dell, Paul Oberlander, David Oliver, J. Paden, Ed Pancreas, Gareth Peddie, Nicholas Peppone, Markus Rausch, Travis Reed, Ellen L. Rosen, Terry Rotter, A. J. Rubenking, Kristin Rupert, Colette Russen, Patricia L.

Kölb, Bev Kutnick, David Lachance, Andrew Lacker, Brian Laik, David Lean, Jeff Lentz, Saren Leono, William A. Marcolongo, Susan J. Marier, Ben McDaniel, John McKenzie, Bob Melton, Rick Miller, Les Mims, Patricia Munro, Dunlap, N. M. J. P. Nacy, Julie Nichols, John Novellino, Don O'Dell, Paul Oberlander, David Oliver, J. Paden, Ed Pancreas, Gareth Peddie, Nicholas Peppone, Markus Rausch, Travis Reed, Ellen L. Rosen, Terry Rotter, A. J. Rubenking, Kristin Rupert, Colette Russen, Patricia L. Rutherford, Colin Ryono, Phillip Schwimmer, Gene Sentowski, Betty Shaw, Margo Sheet, Steven Silverman, John Sledge, Bob Smith, Matthew Smith, Morris D. Sullivan, Bernard J. Sussman, Kiku Terasaki, Bill Thomas, Larry Thornton, Brian Tomarchio, Ulises Tomayo, Sara Uehlein, Alejadra Valencia, Stephen Vekovius, Richard M. Von Essen, Eric Wallace, Bill Warren, Tom Welch, Liam Wescott, Bruce Wolper, Nancy L. Wright, Rick Yaeger.

FILM INDEX